THE ART OF MANAGING MANAGERS

Neil R. Sweeney

National Training Director
Paul Masson Vineyards
Saratoga, California

ADDISON-WESLEY PUBLISHING COMPANY, INC.
Reading, Massachusetts
Menlo Park, California • Don Mills, Ontario • Wokingham, England • Amsterdam
Sydney • Singapore • Tokyo • Mexico City • Bogotá • Santiago • San Juan

Library of Congress Cataloging in Publication Data

Sweeney, Neil R
    The art of managing managers.

    Includes bibliographical references.
    1. Management.　2. Middle managers.　I. Title.
HD31.S798   658.4'3   80-12993
ISBN 0-201-07644-6

Third Printing, August 1985

ISBN 0-201-07644-6
CDEFGHIJ-AL-898765

Preface

THE PURPOSE OF THIS BOOK

The Art Of Managing Managers was written to assist middle managers in building skills that are unique to their level of management. The middle manager is not a first-line manager and not a top-level manager. Little has been written about the skills needed by a middle manager. Most of the literature focuses on management at all levels and as a result misses the point that middle managers need skills not required at other levels of management. This book presents seventeen skills that are uniquely the middle manager's. The assumption is that a middle manager has competent first-line management skills; as a result discussions of these skills are avoided.

There is a personal element in the book also. As I have seen competent first-line managers whom I helped select become middle managers, it has become very obvious to me that they are engaged in a new learning process; they are involved in learning new skills. This book reflects my efforts to help these managers develop, and it reflects their willingness to help me understand their problems.

Dedication

A special word of thanks is due to Herb Kerman, vice president of Seagrams, and Marty Wolinski, regional manager of Inglenook. Herb read the book and suggested several changes based on his more than twenty years of experience as a middle manager. Marty also read the book and made suggestions, but from the point of view of a new middle manager.

All of the middle managers who took the time to answer the Questionnaire about Middle Management also deserve a word of appreciation, as do their bosses at Seagrams (Walter Haimann), Oroweat (Walter Dryer), Inglenook (Fred La Drue), and Paul Masson (Elliot Fine).

The person who is most responsible for my willingness to express myself in writing is my college English teacher, Msgr. Joseph Bailey. Without his help and criticism many years ago, I am sure I would be reluctant to write for publication.

Some of the thoughts about leading leaders came to me as I led increasingly more assertive and independent individuals—my children Francoise and Patrick. To them, thanks is owed for their tolerance of a father who sometimes forgets that leading leaders is not the same as leading followers.

Neil R. Sweeney

Contents

The Middle-Management Questionnaire

As part of the research in writing this book, a Questionnaire about Middle Management was sent to a representative number of middle managers in four national companies. The results of the questionnaire study are presented here, and the questionnaire itself follows. Replies to each question are listed in order of frequency of mention.

1. *What makes your job different from that of a first-line manager?*

   - Making decisions and setting policies
   - Working through managers and not directly with workers
   - More long-term planning
   - Lack of technical work—more management of people
   - Having to use information provided by others
   - More administrative work—more paperwork
   - More follow-up responsibilities
   - More coordination of activities

2. *What skills do you think a person should have to be promoted to a middle-management position?*

- Organization skills
- Desire to make decisions
- Skill as a motivator
- Leadership ability
- Ability to work through others

3. *What are the three most important management responsibilities you have as a middle manager?*
   - Developing and training first-line managers
   - Planning and reaching goals
   - Providing the link between top management and first-line management
   - Forecasting and reaching long-term objectives
   - Motivating people

4. *What training did you receive for your job as a middle manager?*
   - One-on-one training with boss
   - Workshops, seminars
   - Assuming responsibilities gradually
   - Gaining an advanced degree
   - Learning the job by doing it

5. *What topics would you suggest be included in a training program designed for middle managers?*
   - How to motivate managers
   - How to develop management skills in managers
   - How to manage time
   - How to solve problems
   - How to improve forecasting skills
   - How to delegate effectively
   - How to manage a budget
   - How to plan and organize

Following is a copy of the form used in the study.

QUESTIONNAIRE ABOUT MIDDLE MANAGEMENT

The job of the middle manager is different from those of the top manager and the first-line supervisor or manager. This questionnaire is designed to obtain information about middle management from people like you who are actually performing jobs as middle managers.

1. What makes your job different from that of a first-line manager?

_____

_____

_____

2. What skills do you think a person should have to be promoted to a middle-management position?

_____

_____

_____

3. What are the three most important management responsibilities you have as a middle manager?

_____

_____

_____

4. What training did you receive for your job as a middle manager?

_____

_____

_____

5. What topics would you suggest be included in a training program designed for middle managers?

_____

_____

_____

Thanks for completing the questionnaire!

_____

The Skills of the Middle Manager

MIDDLE-MANAGEMENT SKILLS

Catalogs for management seminars are filled with courses for middle managers. If you were to attend one of these courses, you would most likely find that the skills being taught were first-line management skills. Could it be that middle-management skills are the same as first-line management skills? Both kinds of managers plan, direct, and solve problems involving other people. Yet observations of people in your own organization would not permit you to conclude that all successful first-line managers succeed as middle managers. There must be some differences between the skills of the middle manager and the skills of the first-line manager.

PROMOTION TO MIDDLE MANAGER

"Supervisor of Accounts Payable Promoted to Controller"

"Production Control Manager Named Plant Manager"

"District Sales Manager Becomes Regional Manager"

These headlines announce the fact that a person like you has been promoted to a position as a middle manager. The promotion most likely reflects the recognition that you have been a successful first-line manager. In most instances, success as a first-line manager is the result of having conformed to company expectations and developed skills in managing people using a defined system of planning, directing, and problem solving.

Your first-line management skills allowed you to succeed in a management job, but it was a job with limited independence and support systems. For the most part, as a first-line manager you were expected to implement plans rather than formulate plans. Your planning responsibility usually focused on a small work group and infrequently involved planning for work groups other than your own. As a middle manager, you need a different set of planning skills. As a first-line manager, you directed the activities of workers, not managers. Most workers expect to be directed by their bosses. As a middle manager, you must develop skills in selecting, training, motivating, and evaluating other managers, people who are less willing to be directed. As a first-line manager, most of the problems you solved involved applying a prescribed solution to a defined problem situation. As a middle manager, you need skills to help you solve complex problems with no known solutions. As proud as you are to be a middle manager, you will only be successful if you develop higher-level management skills.

An Example of Differences Between First-Line and Middle Management

The first-line manager in charge of a test laboratory is responsible for seeing that lab technicians conduct the tests according to prescribed procedures within the time limitations imposed by the company, and by using the equipment available. The goals of the first-line manager—to conduct the tests; the resources—specified time, a given number of people, limited equipment; the procedures—those prescribed by the company. The middle manager to whom the first-line manager reports has more freedom. He or she can change the number of tests, the kinds of tests, and, with top-management approval, the procedure for conducting the tests. The middle manager can also transfer a piece of equipment from one work group to another. The procedures used are not limited to those that are currently prescribed, and the resources used by the middle manager are less restricted.

A Department—Not a Work Group

One of the most obvious differences in your job as a middle manager is the size of the group you manage. As a first-line manager, you most likely managed a group of six to ten people yourself. The group managed by a first-line manager is usually referred to as a *work group*. The size of the group you manage as middle manager is likely to involve thirty to sixty people whom you manage through your first-line managers. This group is usually referred to as a *department*.

Your Place in the Company Hierarchy

The classic organization chart would place you below the top-management level and above the first-line management level. This placement offers few clues as to the actual job you are expected to perform. A much better way to define your job is to study some of the definitions of a middle manager offered in the literature on management.

Under the auspices of the American Management Association, management consultant Emanuel Kay studied the role of the middle manager. The results of his study are reported in his book *Crisis in Middle Management*. Kay identifies middle managers as those who "manage other managers and supervisors. In this role, they appear as sub-functional heads, for example: Manager, Assembly Operations; Manager, Engineering Evaluation; Manager. Northeast Regional Sales" [1]. After defining middle management in this way, Kay goes on to establish the upper and lower limits of this management role. "First line supervisors who primarily supervise non-exempt employees are excluded [from middle management] . . . Heads of major functional areas . . . Chairman of the Board, President, Executive Vice President and Group Vice President [are excluded from middle management]. Division General Managers who have profit and loss responsibility [are also excluded]"[2]. Top-level managers are those managers who have the overall responsibility for running an organization, which middle managers do not have.

The Need to Change

If you try to continue to function as a middle manager the way you did as a first-line manager, you will find you have an impossible job. There is not enough time in a day for you to develop detailed plans for your first-line managers the way you most likely did for your workers. The limits of your own energy will force you to let your first-line managers direct the activities of their own groups. It is not possible for you to give orders and direct the activities of all of the individuals in your department. Too many problems will go unsolved if you insist on solving all of them yourself. You must trust your first-line managers to solve some of the problems, and limit the number you solve yourself. If you continue to function as you did when you were a first-line manager, you can expect significant *time management* problems. In order to change the way you function, you need to develop the skills of an effective middle manager.

THE KEY TASKS OF THE MIDDLE MANAGER

You can most easily identify middle management skills by examining the key management tasks of planning, directing, and problem solving at each level of management. While all managers perform these tasks, the skills involved in performing them vary at each level.

An Example—Planning in a Printing Plant

A great deal can be learned about the management task of planning by observing managers in a printing plant. The first-line manager schedules the work and oversees the operation of the presses. The middle manager coordinates the work flow from the copy department to the binding department and is also involved in contingency planning when presses are down or material is unavailable. Top management focuses on reaching overall company goals and seeing that interdepartmental plans are being carried out.

PLANNING AS A MANAGEMENT TASK

Your planning task as a middle manager differs from the planning tasks of first-line managers and top-level managers. The information you use, the way you set goals, the types of resource allocations you make, the kinds of strategies you develop, and the types of schedules you establish make your planning task different from planning tasks at other levels of management.

The similarities and differences in the planning task at each management level are outlined in Chart 1.1. A self-rating scale follows.

Using Information

The first-line manager personally collects most of the information used to formulate plans. The accuracy of information obtained from others can be checked at the work scene. As a middle manager, you formulate plans using information provided by others. Because of your distance from the work scene, only rarely can this information be verified easily. The source of information you use and your ability to verify the information used in formulating plans set your middle-management role apart from that of first-line management.

Setting Goals

Unlike the first-line manager, you must focus on both long-term goals and short-term goals. In addition, you must set goals that involve several tiers of people; the work groups as well as department-level staff personnel. Setting long-term and multi-tiered goals differentiates goal setting in these two levels of management.

Allocating Resources

You have greater control over the resources used to reach goals than most first-line managers have. Assigning personnel to new

CHART 1.1 PLANNING TASKS AT VARIOUS MANAGEMENT LEVELS

MANAGEMENT TASK	Management Level		
	Top	Middle	First-Line
Using information	Depends almost always on information provided by others.	Collects some information, but gets most information from others.	Collects most information. Can verify information at work scene.
Setting goals	Focuses on long-term corporate goals. Sets goals for the company based on the purpose of the company.	Focuses on long-term goals while reaching short-term goals. Sets goals for department using company goals.	Focuses on short-term goals; single-tiered goals. Sets goals for work group based on department goals.
Allocating resources	Is free to change the way people are organized. Secures funds for owner/investor to support activities in the company.	With approval of top-level manager, changes the way people are organized. Approves funds within the limits of an approved budget.	Points out need to change the way people are organized. With approval, may change a procedure. Spends funds with the approval of middle manager.
Developing strategies	Precedent may determine what one job is, but how it is done can be changed easily.	Priorities of top-level managers determine what is done, but there is some freedom. Originates new and different strategies.	Procedures determine much of what is done and how it is to be done.
Establishing schedules	Reviews department schedules to see that company goals are met on time.	Reviews work schedules to see that they are compatible. Coordinates department schedules with affiliated departments.	Develops schedules for people in work group to assure that goals are met on time.

6

RATE YOURSELF ON THESE MIDDLE-MANAGEMENT PLANNING SKILLS

Planning Skills	Lacking	Needs Improvement	Adequate	Well Developed
Using secondary sources of information				
Assigning your own priorities to goals				
Formulating creative strategies to reach new goals				
Allocating and re-allocating resources; changing the way a department is organized				
Developing schedules for long-term, multi-tiered plans				
Developing contingency plans				
Coordinating plans with other managers				

functions, redesigning their jobs, and purchasing or modifying equipment are usually beyond the limits of the first-line manager. Funds are spent for operating and equipment needs only with your approval. The first-line manager's resource allocation task is usually limited by the equipment used in the work group. Resource allocation and control for the first-line manager is usually quite limited. While expected to point out the need for reorganizing, the first-line manager lacks the power to effect a reorganization. You are expected to be aware of the need to reallocate resources and to authorize reorganization. You and the first-line manager differ significantly in authority to allocate resources and change the way people within the organization function.

Developing Strategies

Prescribed procedures determine much of what the first-line manager does. The first-line manager has some opportunity to develop alternative procedures, but most typically uses the strategies prescribed by company procedures. You, on the other hand, spend considerable time developing and implementing new and different strategies. Your ability to develop new, alternative strategies for reaching goals is another way you and first-line managers differ.

Establishing Schedules

Schedules for people in the work group are the responsibility of the first-line manager. You, the middle manager, are responsible for ensuring the compatibility of the schedules of the work groups in your department. You must also see that department schedules are coordinated with the schedules of affiliated departments.

An Example—Directing at a Sales Meeting

As an observer in a sales meeting in a district office, you see a district sales manager involved in the management task of directing. This manager urges the sales representatives to reach planned sales goals. The boss, the regional sales manager, is not present.

On inquiry, you learn that the district sales manager is to direct the sales representatives personally. You do find out that the regional sales manager was involved in developing the motivationally oriented meeting outline the district sales manager is using. You also find on inquiry that the regional sales manager's boss, the vice president of sales, approved the sales strategy introduced at the sales meeting. Your observations and inquiries should allow you to conclude that although not present at the meeting, all levels of management are involved.

DIRECTING AS A MANAGEMENT TASK

Your management task of directing includes all of the things you do to see that plans are implemented as formulated. Delegating responsibility for reaching specific goals and evaluating goal attainment are part of your management task of directing. Leadership, which involves influencing other people to do what you want them to do, is also a part of directing. Because it is always possible to improve productivity if people improve their skills, you are responsible for training. When it is necessary to replace people, staffing becomes a part of directing.

The similarities and differences in the management task of directing at each level are presented in Chart 1.2, followed by a self-rating chart.

Delegating

Top management delegates responsibility for department goals to you on an annual basis. In a manner similar to that of the top-level manager, you delegate responsibility for work group goals to your first-line managers. You retain the role of coordinator of work group goals that involve more than one of your first-line managers. By making work assignments or agreeing to work goals, the first-line manager also delegates. The goals delegated by the first-line manager are usually more specific and more limited in scope than those of the middle manager.

Evaluating

Top-level managers usually make formal evaluations of goal attain-

CHART 1.2 TASK DIRECTION AT VARIOUS MANAGEMENT LEVELS

MANAGEMENT TASK	Management Level		
	Top	Middle	First-Line
Delegating	Assign responsibility for department goals on an annual basis.	Assign responsibility for reaching work group goals on a semiannual basis. Assignments are broad and long-term.	Assign or agree to goals for individuals. Assignments are usually specific and limited in scope.
Evaluating	Evaluate performance of middle managers on a monthly basis. The company profit and loss records form the basis of the evaluation. Effectiveness of departments.	Evaluate performance of first-line managers' work groups on the basis of limited but focused observations and written records, usually weekly.	Evaluate performance of individual workers on basis of personal observation of performance; usually on a daily basis.
Motivating	Motivate middle managers who are involved in the process of self-actualization.	Motivate high-achievement, power-oriented first-line managers.	Motivate workers with diverse motivational makeup.
Leading	Lead middle managers by gaining commitment to the company goals.	Lead without stifling the leadership of the first-line manager.	Lead people who generally expect to be led by a leader.
Training	Assist middle managers in developing their middle-management skills.	Help first-line managers develop their first-line management skills.	Train people to perform technical tasks.
Staffing	Select people based on their middle-management skills.	Select people on the possession of or ability to possess first-line management skills.	Select people on the basis of technical skills.

RATE YOURSELF ON THESE MIDDLE-MANAGEMENT DIRECTING SKILLS

Directing Skill	Lacking	Needing Improvement	Adequate	Well Developed
Leading without sti-fling the leadership skills of first-line managers				
Selecting people with current and potential management skills				
Developing management skills of first-line managers				
Motivating high-achieve-ment, power-oriented, determined individuals				
Evaluating the effec-tiveness of work groups rather than individuals				
Delegating permanent responsibility for a work group				

ment at the end of each month. Typically, evaluations are made on the basis of the profit and loss significance of the goals you have reached. Using personal observations and work records, you evaluate goal attainment of your first-line managers on a weekly basis. These evaluations focus on the goals reached and the goals not reached, rather than on profit and loss. First-line managers evaluate individual workers' performances based on extensive personal observation. Evaluations are usually made daily and include a consideration of goals and of methods used to reach the goals.

Leading

Top-level managers tend to assume that you as a middle manager are self-directing, and usually confine their leadership efforts to gaining commitment to company goals and following up on goal attainment. Your leadership role is quite different. You assume that what you do determines the goals your first-line managers will reach. Your leadership dilemma consists of determining how little or how much direction to give. Too little results in lack of goal attainment; too much direction stifles leadership development in your first-line managers.

Training

Development of management skills is the focus of the training efforts of both you and the top-level managers. The first-line manager has a much different training responsibility. That responsibility is to train people to perform technical tasks.

Staffing

Selection decisions are made by top-level managers on the basis of the candidates' possession of middle-management skills. As a middle manager, your chief selection skill is judging the skills of current and potential first-line managers. The first-line manager is usually involved in making selection decisions on the basis of technical skills.

An Example—A Problem with Expense Forms

As you listen to the first-line manager in the accounting department point out the difficulties of processing the newly designed expense form to the boss, you can see something has gone wrong. The people in the work group are having difficulty adjusting to processing the new form. The first-line manager has a problem. On inquiry, you learn that the controller of the company changed the expense form because the other middle managers were complaining about uncontrolled expenses. Middle managers and top-level managers also have problems. You have just observed how problem solving at one level of management can cause problems at another level.

PROBLEM SOLVING AS A MANAGEMENT TASK

If your plans are formulated with complete accuracy and implemented as formulated, you have no problems. Problems develop when something goes wrong (something is not happening that should be, or something is happening that should not be). Managers at all levels need problem-solving skills. Your skills differ from those of managers at other levels in four ways: (1) by the amount and type of information used to spot problems, (2) by the complexity of the problems dealt with, (3) by the necessity of choosing risky solutions, and (4) by the amount of change involved in implementing solutions.

The similarities and differences in the management task of problem solving at each level of management are summarized in Chart 1.3, followed by a self-rating scale.

Spotting Deviations

As a middle manager, you use written and numerical reports to determine whether your plans are being implemented as formulated. Spotting a deviation from your plan involves reviewing extensive verbal and quantitative data. First-line managers typically spot deviations by personally observing the performance of workers or by reviewing their own written records. The amount

CHART 1.3 PROBLEM SOLVING AT VARIOUS MANAGEMENT LEVELS

	Management Level		
MANAGEMENT TASK	Top	Middle	First-Line
Spotting Deviations	Review written and numerical reports of performance and spot deviations from the company plan. Evaluate deviations based on business and industry conditions.	Review written and numerical reports and work group performance to spot deviations from the department plan.	Observe day-to-day performance of workers. Spot deviations from work group plan using observations and records.
Defining the Cause	Consult with middle managers in defining the cause of company problems. Approve middle manager's definition of the cause of the problem.	Consult with the first-line manager in defining the cause of department-level problems. Give approval of first-line manager's definition of the cause of a problem.	Suggest the cause of the problems spotted. Definition of the cause is limited by information available.
Developing Solutions	Develop solutions to company-wide problems. Solutions are limited only by resources available. Approve middle-manager's solutions.	Develop solutions to new and different problems. While solutions are limited to controllable factors, they almost always involve high risks.	Apply prescribed solutions to repetitive problems. Not typically responsible for high-risk solutions.
Implementing Solutions	Approve implementation of solutions that involve more than one department. Depend on others to see that solutions are implemented as approved.	Develop implementation plans for solutions involving department, and propose implementation of solutions involving other departments. Oversee the implementation of solutions that	Personally see that solutions are implemented and develop plans for implementing solutions in work groups.

14

RATE YOURSELF ON THESE MIDDLE-MANAGEMENT PROBLEM-SOLVING SKILLS

Problem-Solving Skills	Lacking	Needing Improvement	Adequate	Well Developed
Spotting problems using extensive quantitative information				
Defining the most probable cause of complex problems				
Choosing risky solutions				
Implementing solutions that involve drastic change				

of information that must be considered in spotting deviations differentiates the middle manager from the first-line manager.

Defining the Cause

Since the activities of more than one work group must be considered, finding the cause of a problem is more complex for you than it is for your first-line managers. You have to consider more information and ask more questions to find the cause of a problem than do the managers who report to you.

Developing Solutions

Solutions the first-line manager develops typically involve applying prescribed solutions to repetitive problems. You are usually involved in developing new solutions to problems that have not been encountered previously. These new solutions are risky solutions to not-so-clear problems.

Implementing Solutions

Because the solutions you implement are characteristically new, you are more frequently involved in implementing solutions that require drastic change. The ability to develop and deal with implementation plans requiring drastic change is one of the major differences between middle management and first-line management.

SUMMARY: THE JOB AND THE SKILLS

As a middle manager, you are the manager who manages first-line managers. Managers at all levels are responsible for planning, directing, and problem solving. There are, however, seventeen skills that set the successful middle manager apart from first-line managers:

1. Using secondhand sources of information

2. Assigning your own priorities

3. Formulating creative strategies

4. Allocating resources

5. Generating long-term schedules

6. Developing contingency plans

7. Coordinating activities with other managers

8. Leading leaders

9. Selecting managers

10. Developing management skills in others

11. Motivating high-achievement, power-oriented individuals

12. Evaluating work groups

13. Delegating permanent responsibility

14. Spotting problems from numbers and reports

15. Defining causes of complex problems

16. Choosing risky solutions

17. Implementing solutions involving drastic change

This book suggests ways of developing each of these middle-management skills.

REFERENCES

1. Kay, Emanuel. *The Crisis in Middle Management.* New York: AMACOM, 1974, p. 4.

2. *Ibid.,* p. 5.

BOOKS AND ARTICLES TO READ

Kay, Emanuel. *The Crisis in Middle Management.* New York: AMACOM, 1974.

Loen, Ray. Sales managers must manage. *Harvard Business Review* 2(3), 111, 1964.

Stewart, Nathaniel. *The Effective Woman Manager.* New York: Wiley, 1978.

CHAPTER 2

Leading Leaders

A LEADER IS A PERSON WHO HAS FOLLOWERS

First-line managers can be called leaders only if they get the people in their work groups to follow them. You can only be described as a leader if you get your first-line managers to follow you. A person cannot be a leader without followers. One of the major differences between the skills of a middle manager and those of a first-line manager is the ability to lead leaders, who are less docile followers.

Leadership involves the approach or style you use to deal with followers. The most frequently used leadership style is the *leader-dominant* or *pressure-compliance* leadership style. While it is possible to succeed as a first-line manager by dominating members of the work group, it is not possible to succeed as a middle manager by making exclusive use of this leadership approach. A more interactive approach is needed if you are to build leadership skills in your first-line managers. This interactive approach is perhaps best described as the *persuasive-collaborative* leadership style. Leading leaders requires skilled use of the persuasive-collaborative leadership style as well as the pressure-compliance style.

A frequently overlooked aspect of leadership at the first-line management level is the mood or morale of the work group. As a middle manager, you cannot overlook this emotional element of leadership. You must sense the moods or feelings of your first-line managers toward you and your department. You must develop positive feeling and a productive atmosphere. Leading leaders involves sensing moods as well as molding moods of the first-line managers and their work groups.

The Roots of Your Leadership Style

The first leader you knew was most likely your father or your mother. The parental figure led—you followed obediently. As you matured, the play group took on increasing importance, and the leadership role was assumed by a peer usually a little older than you. The role of the play group leader most likely was similar to that played by the dominant parental figure in the leader's home. Once again, your experience was with a leader who led and expected you to follow obediently. At school, you were expected to follow the teacher's directions obediently. Your first job most likely was a part-time job in which you were expected to follow the directions of the leader and to do what you were told to do. By the time you were ready to become a leader in the business world, you were most familiar with a leadership style that assumed the dominance of the leader and the dependence of the followers.

Experience as a First-line Manager

The major influence on the type of leader you are today is the result of experience you gained in leading people as a first-line manager. If you got successful results by trusting people, you most likely trust people as a middle manager. If you found that it was necessary to watch people closely in order to get results as a first-line manager, you most likely still watch people closely as a middle manager. If you were successful in getting people to set their own goals as a first-line manager, you most likely still use this goal-setting approach. The experiences you had in dealing with people as a first-line manager greatly influence the way you lead now that you are a middle manager.

THE PRESSURE-COMPLIANCE LEADERSHIP STYLE

The leader-dominant approach to directing activities makes use of direct and implied pressure. The leader gives orders and expects them to be followed without deviation. Those who do not follow the orders or deviate from them risk the wrath of the leader. The leader is feared. Since the leader has power to make assignments and use people, it is possible for the leader to create work conditions that make life unpleasant for those who do not comply. Compliance is demanded. A more meaningful phrase to describe the leader-dominant approach is the pressure-compliance leadership style.

The pressure-compliance leadership style is not without merit. As Leavitt and Pondy point out, the advantages of this style are: "Things get done faster and simple orders can be given" [1]. This method does, however, have a serious disadvantage. The pressure-compliance leadership style makes it difficult for the people following the leader to be anything but followers.

Perpetuation of the Pressure-Compliance Leadership Style

The necessity of getting things done as a first-line manager, and in most instances even the role model of the middle manager to whom you reported, forced you to make frequent use of the pressure-compliance leadership style. You may not have used the power-oriented style exclusively, but you used it frequently. As a result, by the time you were promoted to a middle-management position, you most likely knew how to use the pressure-compliance leadership style skillfully. Since short-term results are the focus of most new middle managers, you may have made too frequent use of the pressure-compliance leadership style. Unless you change and learn to use alternative leadership styles skillfully, you may be perpetuating the pressure-compliance style needlessly.

Middle Managers Do Not Own Subordinates

Leader-dominant models of leadership imply ownership of subordinate managers by higher-level managers. The higher-level manager demands rather than requests actions from subordinates.

The subordinate is summoned with little or no consideration for the resulting inconvenience. This implied ownership is disruptive when used with independent workers in a work group; it is disastrous when middle managers use it exclusively in their dealings with first-line managers. While the leader-dominant style is obviously not the way to build leadership skills in others, the notion still persists that it is "the" way to lead. Myers suggests that "habit, tradition, policy, systems, insensitivity, and introspective myopia" [2] are the reasons for this. Implied ownership builds dependence and hinders subordinates from becoming independent, assertive leaders.

Leadership as a Relationship

The pressure-compliance leadership style assumes that leadership can be defined as a process of directing the activities of followers. It is a definition with some merit, but one with limited scope. An alternative definition is suggested by Hollander in his book *Leaders, Groups and Influences*. Hollander defines leadership as "a relationship between a person exerting influence and those who are influenced" [3]. Accepting this definition permits you to shift from consideration of how a person exerts influence to a consideration of the relationship or interaction between the person exerting influence and those who are influenced. Hollander's definition suggests that the pressure-compliance leadership style is limited because it does not permit the development of an interactive relationship. Leadership can be a relationship in which people influence one another rather than just a relationship in which one person influences and the others are influenced.

THE PERSUASIVE-COLLABORATIVE LEADERSHIP STYLE

Salespeople are noted for their ability to influence other people. The salesperson makes a proposal and then points out to the other person the advantages or benefits of accepting it. The salesperson encourages the other person to ask questions, seek proof and raise objections. The result of this type of approach is that the person being persuaded is involved in the purchase decision. The potential customer is not a silent, compliant follower. Although the salesperson tries to persuade the customer to buy, the decision that is made is the result of a collaborative effort. Because of the collaboration, or interaction, in the decision making the person being sold to is more likely to be committed to implementing the decision. The same approach can be used in leading people.

Rather than use the power of authority to pressure people into compliance, you should depend on the use of the power of persuasion to influence or be influenced. Personal commitment replaces obedient compliance as the moving force. This style of leadership employs the persuasive-collaborative approach.

Your use of the persuasive-collaborative leadership style suggests that the leadership process is the result of a collaboration or interaction between you and your followers. The possibility that a first-line manager is as committed to reaching a work goal as you are is admitted. When you use the persuasive-collaborative leadership style not only do you have the burden of selling or persuading the people you lead to do what should be done, but you let them persuade or sell you on what should be done.

Using the Persuasive-Collaborative Style Skillfully

You begin your learning task by identifying when the persuasive-collaborative leadership style can be used without causing disruption. In his book, *Techniques of Leadership*, Uris [4] points out that the nonautocratic (persuasive-collaborative) leadership style should be used when people are cooperative, experienced, and individualistic. By implication, use of this style with hostile or inexperienced people would be disruptive. The persuasive-collaborative leadership style is also disruptive when compliance is required. In situations where the goal must be reached using specific, prescribed procedures, the persuasive-collaborative leadership style is not productive. While there are limitations on the use of the persuasive-collaborative leadership style, there are many opportunities in middle management to use it.

Preference for Style Is Based upon Assumptions about People

McGregor [5] pointed out in his classic book, *The Human Side of Enterprise*, that the leadership style a manager uses is the result of assumptions made about people at work. If you assume that people cannot be trusted, you are more likely to use the pressure-compliance leadership style. If you assume that people are willing to accept responsibility, you are more likely to prefer the persuasive-collaborative leadership style. There are at least seven assumptions which every manager makes consciously or unconsciously about people at work. These seven assumptions can be stated as questions. The questions are

1. Can people be trusted?
2. Are people willing to accept responsibility?
3. Do people work harder when they set their own goals?
4. Is it necessary to watch closely the work people do?
5. Is it necessary to use pressure and coercion to get people to do things?
6. Do people work better with compliments as well as criticism, or is it better to confine your reactions to criticism?
7. Is it possible to get people to help solve work problems?

If you answered yes to questions 1, 2, 3, 6, and 7 and answered no to questions 4 and 5, most likely you will prefer the persuasive-collaborative leadership style. No to questions 1, 2, 3, 6, and 7, and yes to questions 4 and 5 suggest you prefer the pressure-compliance style.

Lack of Business Leaders

Since the widely used pressure-compliance leadership style hinders the development of leadership skills by encouraging dependence, it must be cited as one of the reasons for the lack of leaders in American business today. The overuse of the pressure-compliance leadership style has resulted in a serious lack of leadership skills in those who, by title, are managers. If you want to develop the leadership skills of the first-line managers who report to you, you must develop skill in using the persuasive-collaborative leadership style.

The Possibility of Conflict

One of the consequences of using the persuasive-collaborative leadership style is the possibility that one or more of your first-line managers will openly disagree with you. At times, these disagreements may intensify even to the point of conflict. The possibility that conflict might develop is probably one of the reasons the persuasive-collaborative leadership style is avoided by some middle managers. While harmony is to be preferred to conflict, there are some advantages of allowing conflict to develop.

Myers [6] puts this issue in perspective when he reminds us of John Paul Jones's observation, "From conflict comes change." If all that leadership involved was directing people in a repetitive, unchanging situation, there would be little need for the persuasive-collaborative leadership style. The persuasive-collaborative style allows middle managers and first-line managers to deal with change.

Conflict can result in productive changes if the managers involved in the conflict search for a solution to the conflict rather than try to prove each other wrong. In their new book, *New Ways of Managing Conflict*, Likert and Likert [7] suggest that a win-win approach to resolving conflict can result when each person involved tries to understand the other person's point of view. The objective of such an approach is to find a solution rather than to prove the other person wrong.

The win-win approach might require you as a middle manager to understand the point of view of the first-line manager and attempt to resolve conflict by finding a mutually agreeable solution. Allowing your first-line managers to disagree with you and to express their opposition openly is one way that both you and they can resolve conflicts and bring about constructive change. Leadership is based on your ability to deal with change.

The Possibility of Commitment

The other possibility that results from the use of the persuasive-collaborative leadership style is the possibility of commitment. Commitment is the process by which a first-line manager becomes involved in reaching work goals. Discussion of the work goals and of the alternatives for reaching work goals makes it possible for a person to become involved in a consideration of these goals and results in a greater commitment to reaching them. The reality of the work world is that first-line managers work harder to reach goals to which they are personally committed. The process of collaboration in which you work with first-line managers to design work tasks and set goals ensures the involvement of your first-line managers. The result is their commitment to reach goals, a commitment that does not result from the pressure-compliance leadership approach. Leavitt and Pondy [8] point out that commitment is the major benefit of the persuasive-collaborative leadership style.

Using Both Leadership Styles

The exclusive use of the leader-dominant, pressure-compliance leadership style may get results, but it will not build the leadership skills of the first-line managers who report to you. The fact that the first-line managers you lead are competent, experienced, and individualistic, as well as the fact that some of the situations you face are not repetitive, suggests that you make use of the persuasive-collaborative style as well. With the use of the persuasive-collaborative style, there is the possibility that conflict will erupt, but there is also the possibility that commitment will result. Conflict and commitment are both necessary if the first-line managers' leadership skills are to be developed and you are to be totally effective as a leader of leaders.

LEADING LEADERS INVOLVES MOLDING MOODS.

Leading leaders requires the use of both leadership styles discussed in preceding sections. It also requires the sensing and molding of department moods and the moods of your first-line managers. A mood is the general feeling first-line managers have toward you and your department. Molding your department's moods requires your awareness of emotionally toned issues.

Positive and Negative Moods

Mood or morale is the result of emotional experiences or feelings accumulated daily in a department. If your first-line managers experience repeated frustrations and continuous failure, they accumulate negative feelings. When these negative feelings are associated with being a member of the department, department morale is negative. This is not to suggest that struggle and difficulties produce negative moods. Struggle, as long as there is a chance for success, or anger, as long as it is directed at the difficulties, can result in positive moods and productive effort. Positive moods characteristically result from experiences of success. If your first-line managers feel they are being helped by working in your department they are likely to have positive feelings toward the department.

Detecting Positive Moods

Because moods involve emotions, it is not always easy to detect them. There are, however, five obvious signs of positive or productive moods in a department:

1. Unwillingness of managers in a department to give up hope and turn against the departmental manager in times of trouble and change

2. Demonstrated pride—the feeling that the department and its people are better than similar departments

3. Expressed appreciation for the benefits derived from working in the department

4. Participation in departmental contests or incentive programs and satisfaction derived from departmental activities, such as meetings

5. Determination of managers in the department to succeed, not to give up

Molding Moods

Using these five indicators, it is possible for you to evaluate the mood in your department. If you find department mood or morale is not as positive as you would like it to be, you can mold more positive moods by doing just three things:

- Building feelings of success
- Watching your own feelings—they spread
- Handling emotionally toned issues carefully

Building Feelings of Success

You can build feelings of success by encouraging your first-line managers to reach goals that are achievable. Goals should be set on the basis of each person's ability rather than by assigning the same goal to each first-line manager. Continued success can be ensured by helping when you are needed and by recognizing success when it is achieved. If you do not recognize and comment on your first-line managers' successes, you have lost the opportunity to build positive feelings and bolster department morale.

Watching Your Own Feelings

The mood in a department frequently is a reflection of your own feelings. If you are tense or discouraged, the managers who report to you will pick up your feelings, and your negative mood may well spread to them. If you demonstrate enthusiasm and optimism, it is likely to spread to your managers. You, yourself, are a mood setter.

Handling Emotionally Toned Issues

Department mood is also affected by the way you deal with emotionally toned issues. An example of an emotionally toned issue is that of demotion. Exhibiting a cold, inhumane attitude while informing a first-line manager that he or she is demoted may be efficient, but it results in resentment and anger. This resentment and anger may spread to others, resulting in low department morale. To describe an obvious error as stupid publicly creates embarrassment and results in negative feelings or moods. To point out an error privately and suggest that the manager try another way results in positive feelings and positive morale. The way you handle emotionally toned issues involving your managers sets the mood for the entire department.

SUMMARY: LEADING LEADERS

Leadership implies the existence of followers. The major difference between leading in a department and leading in a work group is the followers' willingness to be led. As a result, leading leaders as a middle manager requires that you be skilled in using the persuasive-collaborative leadership style and the pressure-compliance leadership style. The reason you must develop the persuasive-collaborative leadership style is that it is the only style that results in followers acquiring leadership skills. Leading leaders also involves greater responsibility for sensing and molding the moods or morale of your first-line managers. Positive morale results in a more effective department than negative morale or moods.

REFERENCES

1. Leavitt, Harold, and Pondy, Louis. *Readings In Managerial Psychology*. Chicago: University of Chicago Press, 1964, p. 370.
2. Myers, M. Scott. *Every Employee a Manager*. New York: McGraw-Hill, 1970, p. 32.
3. Hollander, Edward. *Leaders, Groups and Influences*. New York: Oxford University Press, 1964, p. 1.
4. Uris, Auren. *Techniques Of Leadership*. New York: McGraw-Hill, 1964 p. 30.
5. McGregor, Doug. *The Human Side Of Enterprise*. New York: McGraw-Hill, 1960.
6. Myers, *Every Employee*, p. 27.
7. Likert, Rensis and Likert, Jane. *New Ways of Managing Conflict*. New York: McGraw-Hill, 1976, p. 4.
8. Leavitt and Pondy, *Readings*, p. 370.

CHAPTER 3

Keeping Informed Despite
the Distance

THE CONSEQUENCES OF DISTANCE

One of the big adjustments you have to make as a middle manager is to recognize the fact that you are too distant from the work scene to have first-hand information. You must, therefore, use secondary sources of information. The production manager no longer sees units being produced; the controller no longer watches as bills are paid; and the regional sales manager no longer observes sales being made. Because you are at a distance from the action, you are usually denied direct access to primary sources of information.

As a first-line manager, you typically used information that you personally collected or generated. As a result you were most likely quite confident in using this information to plan, direct, and solve problems. Even when you used information provided by others, you could see with your own eyes the practical implications of using the information. This closeness to the work scene allowed you to have considerable confidence in using the available information.

In most situations as a middle manager, you use information that other people generate. Since you have department responsibilities rather than work group responsibilities, it is difficult for you to observe directly the implications of using information. Production control records, accounts payable portfolios, and sales records are the sources of information for the middle manager more frequently than first-hand observations. You use this information with some apprehension, and rightly so.

An Example—Using Second-Hand Information

A production manager was asked recently to decide whether to increase the number of workers in a work group. Since the recommendation had to be made immediately, the production manager searched for information on the subject. She found three sources of information: (1) a report on the need for additional workers written by the first-line manager, (2) a job description for the workers written by a wage and salary grader, and (3) a work output study prepared by an industrial engineer. Because of time limitations, the production manager never had a chance to make an in-depth study of the workers personally. The recommendation had to be based on secondary sources of information: the written report, the job description, and the work output figures.

The production manager used these three sources of information and recommended that the number of workers be increased. She used the information with considerable apprehension. Her apprehension was based on the realization that the information in the first-line manager's written report most certainly was slanted toward proving the need for additional workers. Because the job description was written with the input of a first-line manager who was interested in getting more money for the workers on the job, it may have contained some overstated complexities. Since the original purpose of the work output study was to demonstrate decreasing productivity to the union, the figures were most likely understated. Despite the questionable validity of the information, these three second-hand sources of information were used, and a recommendation was made based upon them.

VALIDATING INFORMATION

Since you must use information in everything you do, your effectiveness is greatly determined by the availability of valid information. If you presume the validity of all of the information available to you, you most likely will make some critical errors. If you insist on having information with proved validity, you most likely will do nothing. If you try to validate personally all of the available information, you will be so busy proving validity that you will have little time to use it. Unless you want to be ineffective, you need a method of efficiently and quickly validating information.

Validating Information in a Document

There are four techniques you can use to validate information in a document.

1. Determine the original purpose of the document.

2. Look for internal consistency in the document.

3. Check out one part of the document in detail.

4. Review inferences with a person on the scene.

Determining the Original Purpose

Determine the original purpose for which the information in the document was gathered or generated. If the purpose is at odds with the purpose for which you want to use the information, get new information or look for a different source.

Looking for Internal Consistency

Search for incompatible information within the document. Too much incompatible information may suggest that the document is invalid and unusable.

Checking Out One Part in Detail

Check out some of the information in the document in detail. In checking the details of one part of the document you may find inaccuracies that suggest the whole document should be discarded.

Reviewing the Inferences with a Person on the Scene

Check the inferences you make from the document with the person who was the source of the information in the document. Do not review all of the information, just check the inferences; you may find you overlooked some important information in making the inferences.

This method of validating information can be used with all of the documents you use in planning, directing, and solving problems. It is as applicable to computer reports as it is to written reports. While this method will not remove all of the uncertainties of using information you yourself have not collected, it will increase your confidence.

LIVING WITH COMPUTER REPORTS

In the simpler world of the past, information was manually recorded and manually tabulated. In the computer-dominated work world, information is recorded and tabulated by machine. The major difference between these two recording and tabulating systems is that the managers involved in the manual tabulation had greater control over when the reports were generated and were able to correct errors faster when they spotted them. Understandably, some managers do not like to use information on computer reports because they do not get the reports on time or they feel the reports contain erroneous information. Admittedly, it is possible that computer reports lack timeliness and that they do contain some inaccurate information. On the other hand, it is possible that the lack of timeliness can be corrected and that the computer-generated reports are as accurate or more accurate than manually tabulated reports.

Information-Gathering and Decision-Making Reports

The two general types of computer reports are (1) information-gathering and analysis reports and (2) decision-making reports. Information-gathering and analysis reports are computer reports in which information is collected and used to make quantitative comparisons. For example, the actual size of accounts receivable compared to the forecasted size. In decision-making reports, information is used to suggest the choice of one of several actions. For example, information on sales of a brand are tracked. Three alternatives are considered: increasing advertising, decreasing advertising, or continuing current advertising. And one is chosen—in this case, the continuing of the current spending levels because information indicates sales are on target.

Verifying the Input

There seems to be little question that information-gathering and information-analysis reports are useful. Computers and business machines collect information and store it, and they add, subtract, multiply, and divide better than manual tabulators ever did. The only limitation on the confidence you may have in these reports is the accuracy of the information put into the machines. A brief conversation with the people responsible for providing the input information to the key punch operators should help you establish the credibility of the information in this type of report. Show the person who generates the information the actual computer report and ask for verification of the accuracy of the information.

Verifying the Assumptions in Decision-making Reports

Computer reports that suggest planning alternatives and problem solutions may have accurate information but be based upon the wrong assumption and on the wrong planning alternatives and possible solutions. The process of verifying this type of computer report is more complex.

While the number of these computer reports prevents you from verifying the assumptions in each of them, an interesting approach to verifying the most frequently used report might be (1) to gather the information needed to make the decision without using the computer, (2) to use this information to define the problem or state the goal, (3) to develop alternative solutions or strategies, and (4) to use the information to choose a solution or select a strategy.

At this point you have gathered the information and made your decisions without the computer. You are now ready to study the assumptions and the criteria for the decision-making model used by the computer programmer. Ask the data processing manager to review with you the assumptions made by the programmer during the design of the original report. If the assumptions and criteria have not changed, you can use the report with greater confidence.

Building Confidence in Computer Reports

Reports generated by the computer or other business machine can be a tremendous help to you as a middle manager, provided you can use the information they contain with confidence. Two ways have been suggested for building confidence and verifying this type of report: (1) check the source and (2) verify the assumptions.

A Readable Book on Computers

Middle managers with doubts about the use of computers and computer reports might well read a book written about computers for those who do not understand them by two people who do. The book is *The Computer Survival Handbook* by Woodridge and Longon[1]. The book is different from most texts in that the authors assume a light, casual, and at times even humorous approach to their subject.

Using Computer Reports

Five rules for using computer reports are

1. Read the written instructions for using the report.

2. Accept the fact that computer reports contain more accurate than inaccurate information.

3. Never disagree with the recommendations made—always disagree with the information upon which they are based and/or the alternatives considered.

4. If you suspect that the information you are getting is inaccurate or that the decisions recommended are incorrect, talk with the data processing manager.

5. If you still cannot accept the information as accurate or the decisions as valid, talk with top management.

GETTING USABLE INFORMATION
FROM WRITTEN REPORTS

Assembling words and numbers on a page, for one reason or another, is a difficult thing for many managers to do. Some first-line managers lack the skills needed to compose a meaningful written report. Other first-line managers are afraid to put things in writing for fear of being wrong. Still other first-line managers realize that putting things in writing results in a sharing of information, which diminishes the power and control they have as long as they possess the information exclusively. Yet getting first-line managers to put things in writing is necessary if you want to get accurate, valid information from them.

Despite the lack of writing skills, despite the reluctance to make commitments in writing, and despite the hesitance to surrender information, it is possible for you as a middle manager to get usable information from written reports. Your task begins by defining the types of written reports you want. The three types of reports usually requested by middle managers are those which ask the first-line manager to (1) present information, (2) recommend a solution, and (3) propose a plan. The usefulness of all three types of reports can be increased if you suggest a way of organizing each type of report. Suggested outlines for each of the three types of report are presented here.

1. *Report to Present Information*
   - Purpose: a one-sentence statement of the purpose
   - Sources: the sources used
   - Summary: a summarization of the information found

2. *Report to Recommend a Solution*
   - Purpose: a one-sentence statement of the purpose
   - Source: the sources used in collecting information
   - Summary: a summarization of the information collected
   - Cause: a one-sentence statement of the cause of the problem

- Explanation: an explanation of why one cause was chosen over the other causes considered
- Solution: a statement of the solution proposed
- Support: a statement of the reasons why one solution was chosen over the other solutions considered

3. *Report to Propose a Plan*
    - Purpose: a one-sentence statement of the purpose of the plan
    - Source: the sources used
    - Summary: a summarization of the information collected
    - Goals: the goals to be reached by the plan
    - Strategy: the strategy recommended for reaching the goals
    - Support: a statement of reasons why one strategy was chosen over the other strategies considered

An Example—Past-Due Reports

Purpose: The purpose of this report is to present a summary of companies in each geographical region with past-due accounts.

Sources: September, 1976 records of accounts receivable.

Summary: Of the 2000 accounts in region 1, 5 have past-due bills of $4000 or more, 6 have past-due bills of $1000 or more. There are no past-due bills in the other regions.

If you want to get usable written reports from your first-line managers, you should begin by specifying the kind of report you want and then suggest an outline the managers can use to organize the information in this report. If in addition you assume a tolerant attitude toward grammatical errors, inappropriate usage of words and incorrect sentence structure, you will get the kind of information you need.

Evaluating Recommendations Made in Written Reports

In evaluating recommendations or advice, you should determine how well the manager has thought through the recommendation.

This can be done by asking the manager to review the alternatives considered and the reasons these alternatives were eliminated from consideration. When you know how the manager has thought through a decision, you can feel more confident that the recommendation is a valid one that is based on an analysis of all of the information available.

When evaluating a recommendation [2]

- Determine the sources upon which it is based.

- Review the alternatives that were considered and rejected.

- Ask for the reasons behind the recommendation.

GETTING INFORMATION FROM FORMS

An alternative to the written report, and one that requires no writing skill at all, is the form. Forms are used by almost all middle managers to collect information; yet many do not realize that the information obtained from a form is determined to a great degree by the design of the form.

A form should be designed so that the person completing the form is aware of its purpose. Titling the form properly is a good way to focus the attention of the person completing the form on the purpose of the form. Titles like "Daily Sales Activity Report" and "Units Produced per Hour" have a more obvious purpose than titles like "Sales Goals" and "Productivity Analysis." An additional way to ensure that the person completing the form understands its purpose is to state the purpose on the form. An example of such a statement might be "The purpose of the Daily Sales Activity Report is to let you report the accomplishment you made in your accounts today to your sales manager." Titles and clear statements of the purpose on the form are the first two principles of designing informative forms.

Minimizing reporting errors is another factor that has to be considered in designing a form. Making a check mark, entering a number, or entering a coded letter are some of the ways reporting errors can be minimized. Giving the person completing the form enough room to make the required entry is another way. When the form requires a person to make entries while working, it should be designed to allow the person to make entries in the same way work is being performed. Single-letter entries and enough room and designing the form to fit the work scene are factors to be considered in minimizing reporting errors in a form.

One of the temptations of designers of forms is to try to get too much information on a single form. The information sought from a form should be limited to the stated purpose of the form. The amount of information sought should never be so great that it takes more than a few minutes to make an entry on the form. An ideal way to limit the information on a form is to insist that forms be limited to a single page. The criterion can then be used: if it doesn't fit on a single page, an additional form or less information is needed.

Designing Information-Retrieval Forms

Here are rules to keep in mind when designing information-retrieval forms:

- Give the form a title that reflects the purpose.
- State the purpose of the form under the title.
- Use single-letter or numerical entries.
- Make the form fit the work scene.
- Limit the form to a single page.

An example of such a form is presented on the facing page.

MAKING USE OF RESEARCH REPORTS

Almost every middle manager makes use of research reports. Research reports are based on controlled observations of some aspect of the work world made by specially trained people. Since research is actually an experiment, the factors that were controlled and those that were not have to be questioned. In fact, the factors that were controlled and the factors that were held constant are the keys to determining the validity of a research report. Information obtained from research reports is usually quite accurate because of the way researchers ask questions and the way they

WEEKLY ACTIVITY REPORT

The purpose of this report is to give you a tool for planning goals at the begin-ning of each week and reporting accomplishments at the end of each week.

Things that must be done this week:

_____

_____

_____

Things that I would like to do this week:

_____

_____

_____

Day	Activity	Purpose	Results
Monday A.M.			
P.M.			

report answers. Inferences made from research reports have to be considered with more caution.

$3 or $15?

A company selling products through grocery stores recently con-ducted a research study of the sales power of floor-display cards that cost $15 and display cards that cost $3. The research report indicated that the $3 display card resulted in as many consumer sales as the $15 display card. If the research study had been properly controlled it would have been possible to infer that the company should not spend the additional $12 for the $15 display card. A closer look at the study indicated the following. Some of the stores using the $3 display card advertised the product and none of the stores using the $15 display card advertised. The product's location in the store, the number of cases on display, and the price of the product were not controlled. Since all of these factors influence the sales of a product from a floor display in a grocery store, no conclusions could be reached.

Perhaps you have a right to expect that the author of a research report know and understand these things and that you should be free to use the research report without hesitation. Experience suggests that this is usually a fair assumption, but questioning the factors that were controlled helps establish the certainty needed to use the results of research with confidence.

The use of research to obtain information is not limited to existing research reports. In most organizations, you as a middle manager can initiate research projects to gain decision-making information. In instances where you initiate research studies, you can influence the methodology as well as the alternatives that are to be considered. Remembering that a research study is actually an experiment helps assure that the information obtained will be valid.

OBTAINING INFORMATION FROM CONVERSATIONS

As a middle manager asking a question, you expect to get informative answers. Unfortunately, as you ask a question, the first-line manager is also asking some questions. These questions typically are

- What answer does this person want to hear?
- What will I gain by giving the information?
- Will the answer I want to give be understood?
- Will I be hurt in some way if I give the information?

First-line managers ask themselves these questions to defend themselves from being hurt. Like it or not, fear is a part of every conversation. In effect, the first-line managers are qualifying you as a receiver and user of information. Realistically, they are fearful that the information provided for you will be used against them. To encourage an open exchange of information,

- Take time to establish rapport.
- Structure the questions ahead of time.
- Ask the right kinds of questions.
- Avoid catch questions.

Taking Time to Establish Rapport

Like all conversations, conversations between you and your first-line managers should be initiated by establishing rapport. Establishing rapport should not, however, overshadow the purpose of the conversation. Soon after meeting or greeting a person, make the purpose of your conversation known and encourage the person to provide the information you need by asking the right questions.

Structuring the Questions Ahead of Time

Whether you are conversing with a first-line manager on the telephone or in person, the questions you ask determine the information you obtain. The most revealing conversations are the result of questions that you as a middle manager have developed before the conversation begins. Thinking through the questions ahead of time helps keep you on track and makes it easier for the person with whom you are conversing to provide you with relevant information. Casual conversations in which questions are developed during the conversation tend to waste time, produce defensiveness, and make it difficult for the first-line managers to provide the information you need.

Asking the Right Kinds of Questions

Certain types of questions tend to elicit more information than other types of questions. When the purpose of the conversation is to determine how people feel about something or to pick up background information of a general nature, ask a *discussion-generating question*. A discussion-generating question is a relatively unstructured question with no limits on the answer to be given; for example, What do you think about. . . ? Do you feel. . . ? Since the objective of the discussion-generating question is to pick up information or another person's opinion or feeling on a subject, the more open-ended it is, the more likely you are to get a honest answer. The *fact-finding question* is another type of question. It is usually more pointed and is designed to elicit specific information, for example, How many? When did you first. . . ? The third type of question is the *probing question*. Probing questions are questions asked to clarify information a person has previously given you; for example, I'm particularly interested in determining why. . . . Ask discussion-generating questions if you are looking for general information; ask fact-finding questions if you are looking for specific information; and ask probing questions if you want to clarify information.

Avoiding Catch Questions

While questions can elicit information, you should avoid asking questions that you know the person to whom you are speaking cannot answer. These questions are sometimes called *catch questions*. Catching first-line managers without information they should have but do not have does little to encourage them to give you the information they do have. If you know the first-line manager does not have the information to answer the question, don't ask the question.

An Example—Using Five Fundamental Questions

The best questioning techniques are those that offer a systematic examination of a situation and allow all of the relevant information concerning that situation to be revealed. An example of such a technique is one used by a regional sales manager to determine the cause of sales losses.

The five fundamental questions are

1. Is the total business up or down, or is it just one or a few products?

2. Are sales up or down in all territories/areas, or in just a few? Specifically, how is business
   - In the college area?
   - In the inner city area?
   - In the suburban area?
   - In recreation areas?

3. Where did business go?
   - To a competitive product?
   - To another size of the same product?
   - To another product produced by us?
   - To a product priced differently than ours?
   - Was loss of business due to seasonal fluctuation?

4. When did the sales loss begin? Was it recent, or has it been a long-term trend?

5. How much have sales dropped off? Was the loss more than can be expected for seasonal fluctuations or about as much as the same time last year?

PREOCCUPATION WITH IMMEDIATE SURROUNDINGS

It is possible to become isolated from the free flow of information if you are preoccupied with your immediate surroundings: the pressing decisions waiting to be made in the "in box," the unanswered telephone messages, the day-to-day secretarial direction, the people waiting to be seen. All of these immediate concerns tend to force your preoccupation with immediate surroundings. If operating your office becomes more important to you than operating the department, your first-line managers will be denied access to you, and the casual exchange of information will be prevented.

YOU CAN'T BE REPLACED WITH
AN INFORMATION SYSTEM.

Several years ago, psychologist Leavitt [3], suggested that wide-spread application of information technology could do away with the need for middle managers. This is only one of many statements that reflect a misunderstanding of the role of the middle manager. It is probably true that a management information system could be developed that would provide top management with much of the information currently transmitted by middle managers. It is also probably true that most of the repetitive problems that first-line managers deal with could be programmed and solved by computers. The middle manager is not simply a conduit of information, but also a user of information. The uses the middle manager makes of information include planning for the uncharted future, directing people in unpredictable situations, spotting new problems, and pointing out solutions that no longer work. Those who say that information systems can replace middle managers are also overlooking the way information can be used to motivate people. The person with the best, most reliable information is the person with the most power. Information can be and is used by middle managers to get things done in an organization; it is a powerful motivational tool. The fact that middle managers use information rather than just transmit it and the fact that information has motivational significance suggest that no matter how advanced the information system, there will always be a place for you in your organization.

SUMMARY: INFORMATION DESPITE DISTANCE

As a middle manager, you need information to plan, to direct, and to solve problems. Because of your distance from the action, you are forced to use second-hand information. This information can be from computer reports, written reports, forms, research reports, or conversations. Unless you as a middle manager wish to function with overwhelming apprehension, you must develop methods for validating the authenticity of the information you use. A procedure that can be used to validate written or printed sources of information is: (1) determine the original purpose, (2) look for internal consistency, (3) check out one part in detail,. and (4) review the inferences with a person at the scene of the action. The validity of information obtained in a conversation is very much determined by the questions asked. The three types of questions that can be asked to elicit information are (1) discussion-generating questions, (2) fact-finding questions, and (3) probing questions. While you as a middle manager must use information that you do not personally obtain, you can have accurate, usable information if you take time to validate the information available to you.

REFERENCES

1. Woodridge, Susan, and Longon, Kenneth. *The Computer Survival Handbook*. Boston: Gambit, 1973.
2. Stewart, Nathaniel. *The Effective Woman Manager*. New York: Wiley, 1978, p. 105.
3. Leavitt, Harold J. *Managerial Psychology*. Chicago: University of Chicago Press, 1972, p. 321.

BOOKS TO READ

Zimny, George. *Methods in Experimental Psychology*. New York: Ronald, 1961.

The "Mores" of Middle-Management Planning

THE "MORES"

First-line managers plan; middle managers plan. Both are involved in long-term planning, contingency planning, resource allocation, planning that involves other people, and formulating strategies. Middle managers, however, develop

- More long-term plans
- More contingency plans
- More creative strategies
- More plans that involve other managers
- More complicated follow-up procedures

The Planning Process

Six steps are essential to the planning process:

1. State the goal to be reached.

2. Consider the conditions that will exist in the future.

3. Determine the resources available to reach the goal.

4. Develop a strategy for reaching the goal.

5. Establish a schedule for reaching the goal.

6. Decide how to follow up to see that the goal is reached.

In one form or another, this basic process is used by planners at every level in business from top-level management to first-line management [1]. The middle manager shares the strengths and weaknesses of top management's planning skills and is helped or hindered by the planning skills of the first-line managers who report to him or her.

PLANNING DEFINED

Planning is perhaps best defined as the process of developing a proposed course of action for use in the future. It is a process; it involves activity; it is focused on the future.

Goals, objectives, and *targets* are words used by planners. Sometimes they are used with precise definitions in mind; sometimes they are used interchangeably. Goals might refer to short-term goals; objectives to long-term goals. Goals might refer to department objectives and targets to work group objectives. The words should probably be used interchangeably to define the "what" of planning.

Strategy, method, program, and *activity* are all words used by planners to describe the "how" of planning. Having stated the goal that is to be reached, it is necessary to describe what must be done to reach the goal. Strategies, methods, programs, and activities explain how the planner sees the goal being reached. The term *procedure* is used to describe frequently repeated strategies, methods, programs, or activities.

MORE LONG-TERM PLANNING

Planning begins with a forecast of the future. Assumptions about the future are combined with historical data and information about current conditions to develop a course of action for use in the future. It is predicting the future that makes planning such a fascinating and foreboding experience.

One of the main differences between the planning you do and the planning first-line managers do is the time frame for which plans are developed. First-line managers typically plan for next month, next quarter, next year; you, as a middle manager, plan for next year, the next two years, and the next five years. The further away the time frame, the more difficult it is to make a valid prediction of future conditions. As a result, you must have or develop skill in predicting the conditions under which goals must be reached in the distant future.

The difficulty managers experience in developing long-term plans is perhaps best understood from an example. A marketing manager who is planning for sales of a product three years hence must base the plan on a forecast of business conditions three years from now. This plan has to be based upon a forecast of general economic conditions, competitive activity, and consumer preferences. Since all of these factors are unknowns, the validity of the plan for sales of a product is limited by the accuracy of the manager's forecast of the future.

Reviewing and Adjusting Forecasts

Since the basic skill of a long-term planner is skill in forecasting the future, you should begin by reviewing the forecasts of economists and business leaders in your industry. Your own experience and assumptions about the future should then be used to adjust these forecasts. The forecast that you finally accept represents the assumptions you have accepted about the future. Using these assumptions you can state your goal, allocate resources, and develop a strategy for reaching the goal. Reviewing forecasts of the future made by knowledgeable people and consciously noting the forecasts you accept is an important first step in long-term planning.

Putting Your Assumptions in Writing

Because the assumptions used in developing long-term plans are frequently forgotten, you should make a written record of your assumptions about the future as you develop your plan. Putting your assumptions in writing makes it easier to make adjustments in your plan when it is implemented in the future.

The importance of putting your assumptions in writing should become clearer as our example is reviewed. In planning the sales of a product three years hence, the marketing manager made the following assumptions:

1. No new, competitive products will be introduced because of the technical uniqueness of the product.

2. A new advertising approach will be developed that is at least as effective as the current one.

3. Prices will continue to rise, despite the economic slowdown.

4. The size of the sales force will remain approximately the same.

If in three years the goals of the sales plan for the product are not being met, one of the reasons might be that one or several of the marketing manager's assumptions were incorrect. The sales force, for example, may have been reduced in size, or a deluge of competitive products may have entered the market. Seeing the assumptions in writing makes it easier to spot the erroneous assumptions and adjust the plan when it is being implemented.

Long-term planning should begin with a review of the forecasts for the future time frame for which you are planning. These forecasts should then be adjusted based upon your own knowledge. The assumptions that you finally accept should be consciously noted and then put in writing.

In predicting future conditions for long-term plans, it is important to

- Review forecasts
- Adjust forecasts
- Make assumptions
- Put assumptions in writing

WHAT TO DO "IF"—MORE CONTINGENCY PLANNING

Because the more distant future is less predictable, you do more contingency planning than most first-line managers. Plans are formulated to deal with assumed conditions. When these conditions change, the course of action must change. If, for example, a plan is formulated assuming labor costs of $10 and a forced settlement might make this cost $12, a contingency plan must be formulated to handle the increased cost of production. The use of lower-cost ingredients or an increase in the selling price are two of the contingencies that can be considered.

Contingency planning includes the development of a proposed course of action for all of the conditions that could develop in the future. Since most contingency plans are never implemented because the conditions that could change in the future do not change, it is possible to overlook the necessity of developing contingency plans. The production manager might well ask, "Why should I take the time to develop a contingency plan for producing the new product without the new equipment when I know the new equipment will be installed on time?" Almost surely, the new piece of equipment will be installed on time. But what will happen if it is not? Some thought should always be given to such contingencies. The benefits of contingency planning are only apparent when the predicted future changes. If just once you have a contingency plan ready to use and use it, you will continue to be a contingency planner.

Flexibility—The First Rule of Contingency Planning

Contingency planning begins with the development of plans that have some flexibility. If you as a middle manager plan on reaching only minimum goals assigned to you, use all of the resources available to you, and schedule activities with little or no room for extra time; you do not have a plan that can be modified. Plans that lend themselves to modification are necessary if contingency plans are to be developed. Plans with flexibility include goals that are beyond the bare minimum, have some resources in reserve, allow for less than optimum time performance, and allow for the use of more than one strategy or procedure for reaching the goal. Flexibility is the first rule of contingency planning.

Contingency Plan Alternatives

The alternatives you should consider in developing contingency plans are to modify the goal, use additional resources, use a different strategy, or allow more time. Contingency planning usually begins with a consideration of the possibility of modifying the original goal. If the consequences of accepting a modified goal are not too great, this is an acceptable contingency plan. The production manager might, for example, consider producing fewer units on the old equipment until the new equipment arrives. When the consequences of modifying the goals are unacceptable, you should then determine whether additional resources can be made available. More equipment, more people, more money are examples of increased resources. Operating the old equipment on an overtime basis is a good contingency plan if additional money can be made available. The payment of overtime requires the use of additional funds. The third alternative, changing the strategy, is the one most frequently used in contingency planning. The goals remain the same and the resources are not increased, but a different way of reaching the goals is developed. A different strategy is developed. The procedure is changed. Developing a contingency plan that involves a new strategy or procedure is difficult when equipment is involved, but it can be done. While operating a piece of equipment at the top rate of speed is an unacceptable procedure under normal conditions, it might be an acceptable procedure if the equipment is to be scrapped when the new equipment is installed. The last alternative is to modify the schedule and allow more time to reach the goal. A contingency plan that involves the use of additional time is a meaningful plan if the consequences of the delay are not too great. Rather than producing a decreased number of units in five days with the old equipment, the production manager could take seven days and produce the full quota of units.

Contingency plan alternatives are

- Modify the goal
- Increase or change the resources
- Change the strategy
- Modify the schedule

MORE CREATIVE STRATEGIES

Typically, first-line managers use strategies that have a proved record of effectiveness and frequently are formal procedures. First-line managers sometimes make the mistake of using the wrong procedure or the wrong strategy, but they typically are not expected to develop entirely new ways of reaching goals. Work methods are sometimes varied and procedures modified slightly, but basic work methods and operating procedures are formulated by someone other than the first-line manager. The task of developing new strategies, new work methods, and new procedures usually falls on you or a staff person who reports to you. The ability to develop new strategies, to conceive as yet untried ways of reaching goals, and to create new methods is a skill you must develop to become a truly effective middle manager.

The process of developing a new strategy is initiated if the original strategy fails to help you reach a goal. If, for example, an advertising strategy is not producing sales, it is time for a new strategy. The search for a new strategy begins with an understanding of the advantages and disadvantages of using the existing strategy. The advantages of a multimedia advertising campaign might be that everybody is reached, and the disadvantages might be that they are not reached with impact. The new strategy should have at least as many advantages as the old strategy and lack some of the disadvantages. In our example, the new strategy should reach fewer people but with more impact. An examination of strategies used by other companies and of strategies you have used in the past will offer some suggestions for new strategies, but the really creative strategies are the result of your own creative thinking.

Creative thinking is the result of two things:

1. Forcing yourself to take time to think for yourself (introspection)

2. Believing that you have the ability to develop new and different ideas (self-sufficiency)

In thinking about the advantages and disadvantages of existing strategies and in reviewing the experience of others, it is possible to develop a new and different strategy if you take time to think and trust yourself. It is rare that the answer to your need for a new strategy will come from outside. Rather, look within for the answer. To return to our example, the new advertising strategy might well be to reach fewer people with more impact and with one medium; advertise only in national magazines and create the kind of impact in these magazines that will make your product memorable. In order to develop creative strategies, you must take time to think and trust yourself.

The Luxury of Resource Allocation

One of the luxuries of middle-management planning is the fact that you have greater control over the resources you can use than do first-line managers. Shifting funds from one project to another, moving people from one work area to another, using more equipment for one project and less for another are all decisions you can make. Usually the first-line manager has more limited resources to work with.

This luxury can also be the source of weakness in middle-management planning. If you rely on shifting resources to bail out poorly formulated plans all of the time, you will find your resources quickly exhausted. The decisions you make on allocation of resources greatly determine your effectiveness. You must develop skill in determining when to shift allocations of resources and when to look for other ways of reaching goals.

MORE PLANNING THAT INVOLVES OTHER MANAGERS

As a middle manager, you consistently develop plans that involve other managers. Some of the involvement is the result of the need for information, and some of the involvement is the result of the interdependence of activities between departments and within departments. For example, a production manager is expected to develop a plan to coordinate the efforts of each of the work groups in his or her department. The efforts of the work group that assembles the product must be compatible with the efforts of the work group that finishes the product. The two work groups are interdependent. The plan involves both first-line managers. The production manager depends on the sales manager to provide information on the number of units to be produced. Whether it is the need for information or the interdependence of activities, as a middle manager you develop plans that involve other managers.

The key to effective planning that involves other managers is the conscious involvement of these managers in the planning process. Explain to the other managers the goal you are trying to reach and ask them for the information you need to formulate the plan. Use the information they provide to formulate a plan and then reduce it to outline form. Present the plan in outline form to the other managers for review and comment. To be sure that the other managers understand the plan, ask questions about the implications of the plan for the managers involved. For example, if the plan you develop calls for more units to be produced than are usually produced in the time allotted, be sure the purchasing department can provide the additional raw materials. Ask questions about the implications. To be effective, the plan must be presented to the other managers in outline form, reviewed, and the implications pointed out. Once you have received their suggestions and comments, finalize the plan. Since one or two managers will almost always be adversely affected by the plan, take time to explain the final plan to the other managers involved.

Planning with other managers requires you to

- Ask for information
- Outline the plan
- Ask for comments
- Point out implications
- Finalize the plan
- Explain the plan

Multi-tiered Planning

Since most of the planning done by a first-line manager involves a single work group, the planning done can be described as single-tiered planning. The supervisor of accounts payable, for example, develops plans for the staff. The planning you do characteristically involves several levels of management (i.e., first-line managers, other middle managers, and top-level managers). This type of planning is best described as multi-tiered planning. To be effective in multi-tiered planning, you must think through the implications of your plans and explain your plans to the managers above, the managers at the same level, and the managers below you.

MORE COMPLICATED FOLLOW-UP PROCEDURES

Follow-up involves some type of measurement of progress toward the attainment of the goal. The more complicated the goal, the more complicated the follow-up. Periodically during the time when the plan is being implemented, measurements of goal attainment need to be taken. The longer the time period, the more checks are needed on goal attainment. The two elements of follow-up are (1) measurements of sub-goal attainment and (2) a schedule for taking these measurements.

The favorite exclamation of a middle manager of some renown is, "Consider it done!" With this statement, the middle manager wishes to dismiss all questions about follow-up and all questions about the implementation of plans. If this manager's record for follow-up and implementation were good, the statement would indeed be reassuring. Unfortunately, the manager's follow-up record is filled with missed deadlines and neglected assignments.

You as a middle manager have to take follow-up measurements. When your measurements indicate that the ultimate goal will not be reached as planned, it is possible to implement a contingency plan. Follow-up allows you to determine whether what you want to happen is actually happening when you want it to happen. Your follow-up measurements are also useful to all of the people involved in the plan. If follow-up is included in a plan, problems can be spotted before they become insoluble. When you develop plans, include a follow-up procedure or you can be assured of failure. As Schleh points out in *Successful Executive Action*, "Many times action bogs down because no one has been assigned or given the responsibility to follow up, to check up on bugs, and to make the method work" [2]. This procedure is part of your role as a middle manager.

MOTIVATIONALLY ORIENTED GOAL SETTING

A plan begins with a statement of the goal or objective to be reached through the use of the plan. Less obvious is the way goals are set or developed. Should the person developing the plan be allowed to set goals without limits or direction? Should the person be given a goal and then be asked to develop a plan to reach the goal? For the purposes of planning efficiency, the more exact the direction given to the planner, the more effective the plan will be.

There is, however, another point of view. This is the motivational point of view. Psychologists state with rare, absolute certitude that (1) managers set higher goals for themselves than others dare set for them, and (2) managers work harder to reach goals that they set for themselves than to reach goals given to them. These two principles suggest that, for greatest motivation, managers should set their own goals.

The usefulness of this information is limited to planning assignments you give your first-line managers. You must either accept the planning assignments given to you by top management or sell top management on taking a motivational point of view.

HELPING THE FIRST-LINE MANAGER
DEVELOP PLANNING SKILLS

First-line managers learn how to plan by planning. The role of the middle manager in helping the first-line manager develop planning skills is to review the plans of the first-line manager once they have been formulated. You can do this by asking the first-line manager the following questions:

- Are the goals of the plan specific and measurable?
- Have any assumptions been made about the future that are likely to change?
- Is the strategy or procedure to be used appropriate and practical?
- Is the schedule of activities compatible with the schedule of

activities for other plans that involve the same people or machines?

- Can the attainment of the final goal be measured as it is being reached?

The first lesson of planning is that "as much as possible" is an unacceptable goal. To be meaningful, a goal must be specific and measurable. As a result, this is the first question you should ask. As stated earlier, plans involve assumptions about the future. One of the assumptions involves the resources that will be available. Resources should not be overestimated or underestimated. An answer to the question on assumptions should provide you with the information you need to check the accuracy of the first-line manager's assumptions. Some first-line managers are unaware of the limitations of procedures and tend to use them inappropriately without varying them. The question on strategies or procedures is crucial to determining the viability of a plan. Compatibility is the key to evaluating the practicality of a schedule. A schedule considered alone might be very practical, but when viewed in light of the other demands in the work group, it may not be. The success of a plan requires that the ultimate goal be measured as it is being reached rather than only after it is reached. Follow-up is necessary if you are to be sure a first-line manager's plans are effective. These five questions will help the first-line manager to formulate better plans and will permit you to feel more confident that the goals of the work group will be reached. Ask questions about goals, assumptions, strategies, schedules, and follow-up measurements.

SUMMARY: MAKE THINGS HAPPEN

Planning allows you to make things happen rather than let things happen! Through planning you set goals, allocate resources, develop strategies, establish schedules, and formulate follow-up procedures. Managers at all levels are involved in these planning activities. As a middle manager, you make things happen by developing more long-term plans, more contingency plans, more creative strategies, more plans that involve other managers, and more complicated follow-up procedures than do other managers. As involved as these middle management activities are, they are preferable to the alternative: letting things happen.

REFERENCES

1. Stewart, Nathaniel. *The Effective Woman Manager.* New York: Wiley, 1978, p. 33.
2. Schleh, John. *Successful Executive Action.* Englewood Cliffs, New Jersey: Prentice-Hall, 1955, p. 35.

CHAPTER 5

Choosing Risky Solutions to Not-So-Clear Problems

THE MAJOR DIFFERENCE

When middle managers were asked in a recent study to identify the major differences between their jobs and the jobs of first-line managers, they cited the complexity of problems they face and the risks they take in choosing solutions as the major difference. The middle managers pointed out that many of the problems first-line managers face can be solved by using proved solutions, and the decisions they make are frequently the result of applying policy guidelines. The problems middle managers face are more complex, less repetitive, and frequently require the development and implementation of new, unproved solutions developed by others.

Solve the Problem; Don't Worry About the Skills.

One of the difficulties in building problem-solving skills is that these skills are typically best tested in a time of crisis. The most difficult problems require that you use your problem-solving skills in haste. As a result, the time when you perceive the need to improve your problem-solving skills is the worst time to learn them. Your focus, your energy in a time of crisis is on solving the problem, not improving problem-solving skills. Problem solving requires speedy thinking, and speed interferes with reflective analysis of skills. There is a way to build problem-solving skills, but it requires an examination of what has been done. It requires an examination of the behavior involved in solving past problems.

"It Tastes Like Kerosene."

The telephone rings and the first-line manager says to the middle manager, "They say our apple wine tastes like kerosene." Immediately, the middle manager begins the problem-solving process. To collect information, he or she asks, "Who is saying it?" "How have you verified the report?" "Are you hearing it from all over the state?" "Is it just in one wine or all of them?" The answers to these questions give the middle manager enough information to identify the source of concern: "It's a fruit-flavored, low-proof wine and the only reports are from Centerville." The problem has been analyzed and described, but the cause of the problem has not been identified. The middle manager thinks of possible causes: (1) the wine was off-condition before it was shipped; (2) the wine was spoiled in shipment; (3) the wine was spoiled during storage. Considering these possible causes, he or she checks them against the information available. If the wine was off-condition before it was shipped, all of the fruit-flavored, low-proof wine made that day would be off-condition. The information available suggests that this is not the case. Only a limited amount of off-condition wine was found, far less than a complete batch. One possible cause has been eliminated.

The most probable cause is one of those remaining: it was spoiled either in shipment or during storage. Both of these possible causes check out with the available information. A decision must be made as to which of the two remaining causes is the more probable cause. The middle manager decides that the more probable cause is the storage of the wine in the local warehouse.

The middle manager immediately begins to develop possible solutions to the problem: (1) store the fruit-flavored, low-proof wine in a new warehouse; (2) build a special storage room in the existing warehouse; or (3) find a way of making the wine so that it will not spoil during storage.

Each of these solutions involves spending money; two of them are immediate, and one is long-term. The middle manager must decide on a solution. The decision has to be made within the limits of the money available to solve the problem. The solution chosen: build a special storage room in the existing warehouse. This solution, like all solutions, requires planning before it can be implemented. Who will be responsible for designing the room? Who will build it? When will the room be ready?

THE PROBLEM-SOLVING PROCESS

The problem-solving process used in the example of the spoiled wine was the familiar four-part problem-solving process. Its steps are

1. Collect information/describe the problem.

2. Consider possible causes/decide on the most probable cause.

3. Develop possible solutions/decide on the best solution.

4. Develop a plan for implementing the solution.

Keep in mind that the problem the first-line manager took to the middle manager did not involve what to do immediately. The immediate solution was prescribed by company procedure. The procedure specified, "Whenever a report of off-condition wine is received, shipments of that wine to stores are to be stopped immediately and all inventory in stores checked." This solution had already been implemented when the first-line manager placed the call to the middle manager.

Problems, Who Has Problems?

A carefree wanderer was once encouraged to talk about his problems. In reply he said, "I don't have any problems. I expect nothing from life and when I get nothing I'm not surprised." Carefree and without goals, the wanderer was telling the truth. Problems only arise when you expect something to happen and it does not happen. Problems only exist in situations where you are expected to reach a goal and you do not reach it. Stewart suggests that a problem should be defined as "anything that is off target ... divergent from whatever was expected"[1]. Kepner and Tregoe define a problem in a similar manner. A problem is "a deviation ... between what should be [happening] and what is actually happening"[2].

When Something Has Gone Wrong

In a problem situation, something has gone wrong. What you planned on happening is not happening or what you planned would not be happening is happening. For you that means that the results or goals you planned on reaching are not being reached. When you realize that something has gone wrong, you should systematically collect all of the available information concerning the situation.

Describing the Problem

The deviation between the expected and what is actually happening is usually caused by a change of one kind or another. The purpose of describing the problem is to gather enough information to identify what change occurred to prevent the expected from happening or to result in the unexpected happening.

The information-gathering process begins with a probe similar to that of the English class composition writer. You should ask the questions Who? What? Where? and When? to get enough information to answer the question Why? This questioning process is almost instinctively used by adults in information retrieval situations. Skill in using this questioning process can be further developed if you write down the questions as you ask them and record the answers as you think them out.

The Questioning Process

The questions Who? and What? identify the problem situation. The location of the problem is determined by the question Where? The time frame is established by the question When?

You can describe problems by asking

- Who?   Identify the people in the problem.
- What?   Identify the factors involved in the problem.
- Where? Specify the location involved.
- When?   Determine the time frame involved in the problem.

A Late-Shipment Problem

The situation: important customers are complaining about late shipments. Questions and answers are necessary:

- *Question: Who is complaining? Answer:* Don's Department Store and Bill's Big Store.

- *Question: What products are being received late? Answer:* Gift-wrapped products.

- *Question: When did the late shipments first begin? Answer:* October 1.

- *Question: Where are these accounts located? Answer:* In the West and Midwest.

After asking these questions and obtaining the answers, you know that the problem has to do with late shipments of gift-wrapped products to the West and Midwest, which are being ordered by Don's and Bill's. Your questions have allowed you to focus on the area of concern: late shipments of gift-wrapped products. Since gift-wrapped products are produced in a different plant from the other products, production problems could be the cause of the late shipments. You also know the problem has something to do with the West and Midwest. Since products are shipped by rail to the West and Midwest and by truck to the East and South, it is possible that the carrier is the cause. A difference has been discovered, and a difference suggests the cause of the problem. But before you jump to a conclusion, more questions need to be asked. Since the shipping problem did not start before October 1, changes that occurred around this time have to be considered. On inquiry, you find that the same order clerk took the order from Don's and Bill's, and the clerk started to work at the plant September 1. You have obtained information by asking questions and making inquiries to describe the problem.

Considering Possible Causes

The same information you use to describe the problem can also be used when you consider possible causes for the problem. Something has gone wrong, and you must discover the cause. By examining the information available you can identify the changes that may have caused the problem. Once you are aware of these changes, you can determine possible solutions.

The cause of the late-shipment problem may have been (1) the production of the gift-wrapped products, (2) the method of shipping the products, or (3) the way in which the orders were processed.

You have identified three possible causes. While it could be that all three factors caused the problem, most likely only one of the causes is the real cause. By examining each of the possible causes against all of the available information, it is possible to eliminate some of the causes and decide on the most probable cause.

Deciding on the Most Probable Cause

Identifying the cause of a problem always requires a choice because identification is a decision based on limited information. You can reduce the odds of choosing the wrong cause by checking each of the possible causes against all of the available information. The process, using the example, can be put like this: (1) if the cause of the problem were production, the late shipments would not have been limited to the West and Midwest; (2) if the cause of the problem were the carrier, then all of the products shipped since October 1 would have been late; (3) the most probable cause of the problem is the new order clerk, who most likely does not know how to process an order for gift-wrapped products. Accepting the order clerk as the cause permits you to explain what happened.

Information is obtained by asking questions. Answers to these questions are thought out and written down. An examination of this information suggests possible causes. These causes are stated and then tested against all available information. Using this process you can identify the most probable cause.

Determining the Importance of a Problem

Some problems you face are worth two hours of your time and some are worth two minutes. Determining how much time to spend on a problem should be based on a judgment of the importance of the problem. Since importance determines the amount of time spent and the degree of involvement, it is really a judgment of what resources you should allocate to solving the problem. Obviously, you should become more involved in solving problems that result in significant financial losses than in those with no losses. Problems that result in serious disruptions deserve more of your attention than those causing minor disruptions.

The off-condition wine problem in the example was complex and costly. It was a problem that only the middle manager could solve because the middle manager alone had the information to do it. The late-shipment problem was simpler and would not have occurred if the first-line manager in charge of the order department had properly trained the new order clerk. The first problem was worth a considerable amount of the middle manager's time; the second problem should have been handled with little involvement of the middle manager.

Developing Possible Solutions

The search for information and the questions asked to this point have been questions about the past. Once the cause of the problem has been identified, solutions can be developed. Solutions focus on the future.

The quality of the solutions developed can be greatly improved when you begin the process by reviewing (1) a statement of the problem, (2) the cause of the problem, and (3) the resources available to solve the problem.

State what you want to happen that is not happening or what you do not want to happen that is happening. Consider the cause of the problem. Determine the resources such as money, people, and equipment that are available for solving the problem. Within this framework, you can develop a solution that is practical and will solve the problem.

An Example—Warehouse Pilferage

The problem: Warehouse pilferage has reached unacceptable limits. The cause: Employees come and go as they please. The resources: $1000. Using this problem statement, this cause, and this financial resource, you can establish a framework for developing solutions. Three solutions that can be proposed to solve the pilferage problem are

1. Hire a detective to find out who is stealing.

2. Design and install a surveillance system.

3. Install locks and make people sign in and out.

The Search for Solutions

The search for solutions begins with an examination of your own experience with similar problems. It should also include suggestions for solutions from other people: your boss, other middle managers, and your first-line managers. Unless you want to be tied to solutions that have been successful with similar problems in the past, you should also consider new and different solutions to problems.

In searching for solutions you should develop as many solutions as possible. This allows for choice and increases the chances that you will choose an effective solution. Too many managers are willing to accept the first possible solution that comes to mind and use it. A much better approach is to develop multiple solutions.

Developing Multiple Solutions

You can develop multiple solutions by

• Thinking beyond the easy solutions yourself.

- Actively seeking out proposed solutions from others.
- Using brainstorming techniques.

Brainstorming The advertising business is famous for the brainstorming technique. In this technique, the advertising problem is outlined to a group of people and they are asked to make recommendations for solving the problem. The brainstorming conference is like all other conferences except that (1) any solution is welcome—no matter how different or ridiculous it might seem no solution is rejected; and (2) no one is allowed to criticize, censure, or make evaluative comments on any of the solutions proposed. The conference is limited to developing new and different solutions. The solutions developed are not evaluated in the brainstorming conference. Effective new solutions can be developed to almost any problem using the brainstorming approach. Fear of proposing new and different solutions is reduced, and one proposed solution suggests another.

Evaluating the Solutions and Choosing the Best

The solution chosen has to solve the problem and solve the problem within the limits of available resources. As a result, each solution has to be evaluated to determine whether the solution really will solve the problem and whether the solution can be used with the resources available.

To return to the pilferage problem, solutions 1 (hire a detective) and 2 (install a surveillance system) would most likely solve the problem, but both solutions cost more than $1000 and therefore are not usable. Solution 3 (install locks and make people sign in and out) costs less than $1000 and is also likely to reduce warehouse pilferage to acceptable limits.

The Fear of Deciding on a Solution

Choosing a solution is almost always a risk for you as a middle manager, since you face few situations where there is only one possible solution. In most situations, several solutions are affordable and seem to be good solutions to the problem. When several solutions are available and all seem to meet the criterion of effectiveness, you must make a subjective and risky choice. All of the decisions involved in choosing a solution are risky; survival in middle management requires an acceptance of this fear. While making the risky choice may open you up to criticism, you are more open to criticism if no solution is chosen and the problem continues.

When to Pass It On

At times the most appropriate thing for you to do is to pass the decision on to someone else; to your boss in top management or to one of your first-line managers. Passing the decision on to your boss is appropriate if none of the alternative solutions can be effected using available resources. Passing the decision to one of your first-line managers is appropriate when it becomes clear that the solutions only involve that manager's work group.

Making Risky Decisions

The complexity of the problems, the necessity of pioneering new solutions, and the irreversibility of your decisions make them high-risk choices. Risk means fear. While this fear can never be eliminated, it can be significantly reduced by taking confidence-building precautions.

Confidence-Building Precautions There are four ways to reduce the fear caused by making risky decisions:

1. Accept the fact that risk-free solutions seldom exist.

2. Consider doing nothing as a solution.

3. Determine the advantages and disadvantages of each solution.

4. Choose the solution with the most advantages and fewest disadvantages.

The Problem-Solving Worksheet

The process that has been suggested for solving problems involves collecting information, describing the problem, considering possible

PROBLEM-SOLVING WORKSHEET

1. The problem: What happened that should not have happened or what did not happen that should have?

_____

_____

2. The questions:

Who is involved?_____

What went wrong? _____

_____

Where is it happening? _____

When did things start to go wrong? _____

3. List possible causes.

1. _____

2. _____

3. _____

4. Which of these causes best explains what went wrong? _____

5. List possible solutions.

1. _____

2. _____

3. _____

6. Decide on a solution. _____

7. Can the solution be used with available resources? _____

8. How will the solution make things happen the way you want them to happen?

_____

_____

causes, deciding on the most probable cause, developing possible solutions, and deciding on the best possible solution. It is a systematic process that lends itself to the use of a worksheet similar to the one presented on the previous page.

The Problem-Solving Process

The process just described has several important characteristics that minimize and reduce the difficulty and increase the probability of finding an effective solution to a problem. This process provides the following:

- Encourages the search for additional information
- Systematically eliminates possible causes and possible solutions
- Makes it possible to visually analyze the steps taken in finding the cause and the solution

Develop a Plan for Implementing the Solution

Once you have decided which solution will be used, you have to develop an implementation plan. The plan should include a clear statement of the goal to be reached, a statement of the method or strategy to be used to reach the goal, and a schedule for reaching the goal. Without developing a thorough implementation plan, there is very little chance that your solution will be implemented. Every implementation plan should include (1) goal/standards (quality, quantity), (2) strategy, and (3) schedule.

HELPING FIRST-LINE MANAGERS IMPROVE THEIR PROBLEM-SOLVING SKILLS

The role of the middle manager in building problem-solving skills in first-line managers is that of a consultant. A consultant is a person who works with others to help them solve their own problems. The consultative approach to developing problem-solving skills in first-line managers builds skills through involvement, not domination.

Build your first-line managers' problem-solving skills by

- Beginning with a review of information
- Discussing possible causes
- Asking the first-line manager to choose a cause
- Reviewing resources and policies
- Asking the first-line manager for a solution
- Assisting the first-line manager in implementing a solution

Beginning with a Review of Information

Begin by asking the first-line manager to review all of the information that is available on the problem situation. If the first-line manager lacks sufficient information, suggest that more be obtained and suggest overlooked sources of information. If the manager has sufficient information, help to organize it so that it can be used to solve the problem. The Problem-Solving Worksheet can be used for this purpose.

Discussing Possible Causes

Using the information available, encourage the first-line manager to develop a list of possible causes. Discuss each of the possible causes and check them against all of the information available.

Asking the First-Line Manager to Choose a Cause

Ask the first-line manager to choose the most probable cause and "walk through" the decision-making process together. If you disagree with the first-line manager's choice, ask him or her to reconsider the other possible causes.

Reviewing Resources and Policies

Once the cause has been accepted, establish what resources are available and what policies and procedures are involved in the problem.

Asking the First-Line Manager for a Solution

Ask the first-line manager to decide on a solution. If the solution to be used is prescribed by company procedures, be sure he or she understands the prescribed solution. If the solution is not prescribed, encourage the first-line manager to draw on past experience and develop several possible solutions without your help. Review all of the solutions together. Ask the first-line manager which solution he or she will use. Review the decision by asking questions. Will the solution proposed solve the problem? Is it consistent with company policies and procedures?

Assisting the First-Line Manager in Implementating a Solution

Having decided on a solution, the first-line manager should then develop a plan for implementing the solution. The plan should include specific goals, a strategy, and a time frame.

SUMMARY: A CRISIS SKILL

Problem solving is a key skill for a middle manager. Because this skill is used in times of crisis, it is important to develop a systematic approach to solving problems. The approach recommended includes (1) collecting information, (2) describing the problem, (3) considering possible causes, (4) deciding on the most probable cause, (5) developing possible solutions, (6) deciding on the best possible solution, and (7) developing a plan to implement the chosen solution. As a middle manager you face problems that are complex, and the financial implications of the solutions you decide to use are significant enough so that you will always be in a fear-producing situation. It is a situation in which you must choose risky solutions to not-so-clear problems.

REFERENCES

1. Stewart, Nathaniel. *The Effective Women Managers*. New York: Wiley, 1978, p. 124.
2. Kepner, Charles H., and Tregoe, Benjamin B. *The Rational Manager: A Systematic Approach To Problem Solving And Decision Making.* New York: McGraw-Hill, 1965, p. 47.

CHAPTER 6

Motivating High-Achievement, Power-Seeking, Determined Individuals

PLANS, SOLUTIONS, AND PEOPLE

There has yet to be a plan formulated by a middle manager or a solution implemented by a middle manager that does not involve other people in some way. When plans are being formulated and solutions considered, you make the assumption that people can be made to perform in a given way. You make the assumption that you can get your first-line managers to do what you want them to do. Getting people to do what you want them to do is what motivation is all about.

WHAT MOTIVATES FIRST-LINE MANAGERS

The simplest rule of motivation is: know the individual you are trying to motivate. This simple rule becomes complex when the reasons why first-line managers do things are considered. The reasons why they do things are referred to as *motives*. According to psychologists, motives include *needs, shapers,* and *goals* [1].

Freud suggested that people do things for a reason—because they have a need. He also contended that individuals are not always conscious of the needs they are trying to satisfy. Because he was first trained as a physiologist, Freud suggested that people do things to satisfy physical needs such as sex. Others rejected Freud's emphasis on the physical needs and pointed out that psychological needs such as acceptance and approval are important motivational forces. Physical and psychological need satisfaction helps explain why first-line managers do some, but not all, of the things they do.

Other psychologists suggest the existence of shapers of human behavior such as values. These motivational forces are more permanent determiners of what people do and they shape the way needs are satisfied.

Similar to shapers but operating on a conscious level are goals. Goals are personal objectives a person consciously wants to reach.

Understanding the motivational makeup of first-line managers requires an examination of these three motivational forces. They are further clarified in Chart 6.1.

CHART 6.1 THE THREE MOTIVATIONAL FORCES

MOTIVATIONAL FORCE	DEFINITION
Needs	The physical and psychological forces within a manager that result from the absence of something that is needed for the well-being of that manager.
Shapers	The forces within a manager, such as values, interests, and attitudes, which determine how needs are satisfied.
Goals	The need-satisfying objectives that a manager consciously tries to reach.

NEEDS

Physical and psychological need satisfaction helps explain why first-line managers do some of the things they do. A list of common needs and their definitions is presented in Chart 6.2.

The list of physical and psychological needs in Chart 6.2 is long. It includes fifteen distinct psychological needs and five phys-

CHART 6.2 COMMON NEEDS

NEED		DEFINITION
Physical Needs		Needs for food, water, sex, rest, and activity
Self-Oriented Psychological Needs	Affection	Need to love and be loved
	Security	Need to feel that one is relatively free from the destructive and threatening pressures of the world
	Status	Need to have feelings of personal worth
	Achievement	Need to accomplish something of significance on one's own
	Independence	Need to function effectively alone with little or no support
	Change	Need to do things in a new and different way
	Endurance	Need to stick with a project despite difficulties and see it to completion
	Growth	Need to become better in some way, to fulfill one's potential
Socially Oriented Psychological Needs	Affiliation	Need to be part of a group
	Social approval	Need to be accepted or respected by a group
	Recognition	Need to have one's own achievements, one's contributions accepted by the group
	Exhibition	Need to express oneself with flair or in a clever or amusing manner
	Power	Need to control the activities of others, to be in charge, to have responsibility
	Aggression	Need to do battle with others, to take on opposition
	Conformity	Need to act in accordance with the rules of the group

ical needs. Each need represents a force within individuals that moves or propels people to do things. An understanding of the meaning of each of these needs will increase your understanding of the motivational factors that influence the first-line managers who report to you.

The need to have feelings of personal worth (status) helps explain the fight for the best office. The need for affiliation makes membership in social and civic organizations a bit more meaningful. The need to feel free of the threatening pressures of the world partly explains why a manager is overly cautious.

The Strength of a Need Can Change

The strength of a need is not constant. Experience and environmental conditions can influence the strength of a need. First-line managers may have strong need for independence when they begin their jobs but, after repeated frustration of all attempts to satisfy the need at work, the need may weaken or be satisfied outside work. Conversely, first-line managers may have a weak need for affiliation when they first join the company but, after repeatedly pleasing experiences resulting from group membership, the need is strengthened. Needs change as a result of experience and environmental conditions.

The Strength of the Need Establishes Individuality

While every person has each of these needs, the strength of the needs varies considerably from person to person. Some managers have a great need for security; others, a lesser need. Some managers have a great need for power; others, a moderate need. It is because the strength of each need varies that it is possible to use needs to get people to do what you want them to do. Variability establishes individuality.

HIGH-ACHIEVEMENT, POWER-SEEKING, DETERMINED INDIVIDUALS

The typical profile of the strength of each need in a successful first-line manager is shown here.

Strength of Need	Need
Low-medium	Affection
Low-medium	Security
Low-high	Status
High	Achievement
High	Independence
Medium-high	Change
High	Endurance
High	Growth
Medium	Affiliation
Low-medium	Social approval
High	Recognition
Medium-high	Exhibition
High	Power
Medium-high	Aggression
Low-medium	Conformity

Because first-line managers characteristically have high needs for independence, endurance, achievement, recognition, and power they can be described as high-achievement, power-seeking, determined individuals.

Needs Are Revealed by Words and Actions

If you are a perceptive observer, you can learn a great deal about the motivational makeup of your first-line managers just by watching them at work and listening to what they say. The first-line manager with a strong need for achievement will talk excessively about wanting to do things well, wanting to be better than anyone else. The high-achievement manager is the one who volunteers to do things that will provide an opportunity to outperform peers. This person is constantly looking for ways to improve personal performance and the performance of the people in the work group. The manager with a weak need for independence asks for excessive help, seeks assistance and frequent reassurance. A need that is particularly evident from observation is the need for power. The manager with strong needs for power looks for opportunities to have an impact on other people and is particularly interested in trying to influence, persuade, make a point, and impress people. This person talks a great deal about past successes that are due to his ability to control the behavior of other people. Through observation, you can determine the strength of the fifteen psychological needs in each of your managers.

SHAPERS

Greatly influencing the way a first-line manager satisfies needs are a group of motivational forces called shapers. Shapers include interests, attitudes, and values.

An *interest* is a relatively permanent tendency to respond to or get involved in certain kinds of activities. Some of the interests that have been studied in the past and are still relevant are: (Kuder[2])

- Interest in numbers
- Interest in mechanical things
- Interest in things scientific
- Interest in persuading others
- Interest in artistic activities
- Interest in helping other people
- Interest in matters involving details

The usefulness of knowing a first-line manager's interests can be seen when applied to the way he or she might satisfy a high need for achievement. A manager with a strong interest in numbers would tend to satisfy the need for achievement by excelling in the quantitative aspects of the job. A manager with strong interests in persuasive activities would tend to satisfy the need for achievement by excelling in getting others to agree.

An *attitude* is a relatively permanent tendency to view some aspect of life in a set way. Attitudes that are typically studied in motivational research are attitude toward work, attitude toward authority figures, and attitude toward workers. A first-line manager who views work as an enjoyable experience will approach

work with a different frame of mind than a manager with a negative frame of mind. Hostile attitudes toward authority figures
usually result in first-line managers trying to satisfy basic needs in
opposition to their bosses. Attitudes determine how the world is
perceived by individuals. Once attitudes are formed, they are difficult to change. Because they resist change and shape perceptions,
attitudes impose limits on how needs can be satisfied.

A *value* is a relatively permanent tendency to view certain
things as being particularly good, valuable, or prized. The values
that have been isolated and studied are theoretical, economic,
aesthetic, philanthropic, political, and religious. A manager with
strong theoretical values prizes activities that allow a search for
the truth, discovery of new and different things. This type of manager would be happiest affiliated with groups of people having
similar theoretical values. A manager with strong aesthetic values
would seek out activities that allowed satisfaction of recognition
needs by involvement in activities that require grace and symmetry
(Alport, Vernon, Lindsey[3]).

Interests, attitudes, and values help shape the way a manager
satisfies basic needs. As such, they must be considered in determining the motivational makeup of a first-line manager.

GOALS

A goal is something a first-line manager consciously wants or seeks,
something a manager wishes to become or an objective that is so
important that it is strived for consciously. Examples of personal
goals that first-line managers might try to reach are a promotion,
maintenance of the status quo, a new house, college education
for children, or a transfer. Personal goals have meaning because of
the needs satisfied as a consequence of reaching the goals. For
example, getting a promotion will most likely satisfy a person's
need for recognition, greater power, and independence. Purchase
of a new house is likely to satisfy a person's need for status as
well as social approval. Myers[4] suggests that goals leading to satisfaction of the needs for growth, achievement, power, recognition,
affiliation, and security have the greatest motivational significance.

Almost anything a first-line manager is asked to do can have motivational significance if it ultimately leads to reaching one of his or her personal goals. Goals have pulling power.

Goals Have Power if They Are Attainable.

While effort is required to reach goals, attainability, or the likelihood of reaching a goal adds motivational significance to a goal. A first-line manager may have a personal goal of getting a Ph.D., but its attainability may be so remote as to give it little meaning. On the other hand, a first-line manager's goal of getting an M.B.A. has great motivational significance because of its attainability on a part-time basis. Personal goals with some likelihood of being reached have the greatest motivational power.

Needs, Shapers, and Goals

Needs are the basic forces of motivation. Needs exist within every first-line manager and move or propel him or her into action. Shapers determine the way needs are satisfied. Goals are the objectives that first-line managers are willing to work hard to reach. The consequence of reaching a goal is need gratification. As such, goals have immense motivational power.

Identifying the needs, shapers, and goals of each of your first-line managers is necessary before you can be a successful motivator. Without this understanding, the research on motivational techniques is difficult to discuss and even more difficult to evaluate. The Motivational Profile presented on the following page is designed to help you identify these motivational factors when evaluating your first-line managers.

MOTIVATIONAL TECHNIQUES

Understanding the motivational makeup of each of your first-line managers will give you a valuable motivational tool. You will know the strength of each of your managers' needs, the way these needs are satisfied, and the short- and long-term goals that give them direction. The techniques of using this information to get

REFERENCES

1. Broadwell, Martin. *The New Supervisor*. Reading, Massachusetts: Addison-Wesley, 1977, p. 19.

2. Sampson, Ray. *Managing the Managers, a Realistic Approach to Applying the Behavioral Sciences*. New York: McGraw-Hill, 1965, p. 210.

3. Coffin, Richard. *The Negotiator*. New York: AMACOM, 1973, p. 89.

4. Kay, Emanuel. *The Crisis in Middle Management*. New York: *AMACOM*, 1974, p. 76.

5. Stanton, William, and Buskirk, R. *Management of the Sales Force*. Homewood, Illinois: Irwin, p. 83.

6. Stewart, Nathaniel. *The Effective Woman Manager*. New York: Wiley, 1978, p. 62.

CHAPTER 9

Selecting First-Line Managers from Within or Without

"WANTED: FIRST-LINE MANAGER"

One of the most challenging moments in your life as a middle manager is when a new first-line manager must be found. It is challenging because it can make or break you. If your choice is a good one, you will be more effective. You will be able to delegate more and get more accomplished. If your choice is a poor one, if the person chosen either lacks the management skills or fails to actualize his or her potential in the new situation, you, the middle manager, will be performing two jobs, yours and the first-line manager's. As a consequence, the task of selecting a first-line manager transcends the simple announcement "Wanted: First-Line Manager."

ANALYZING THE JOB

Since you are responsible for selecting the first-line manager, you must define the kinds of skills required for the position. Candidates from within the company and candidates from outside the company can only be evaluated if you have defined the skills needed. The process of defining the skills needed to perform a job is called a *job analysis.*

While conducting a job analysis is not simple, it can be done with a limited amount of effort. When one middle manager was asked recently how he determined the skills needed to perform a first-line management job, he answered, "I begin by looking at the job description; next I take a look at the performance evaluations of people in the job and in similar jobs, talk to a few people in these jobs, and then make up my own mind as to the skills needed to perform the job." The process he described is the job analysis process.

Conducting a Job Analysis

A job analysis begins with a statement of the goals of the job, followed by observations made by people performing the job, conversations with people performing the job, and discussions about the job by the managers of the people in the work group. After the information is obtained, it must be analyzed, and generalizations must be made about the skills needed for the job. To perform a job analysis effectively, it is necessary to:

- Develop a statement of job goals.
- Make on-the-job observations.
- Discuss the job with others.
- Analyze and generalize.

A job analysis begins with a statement of the goals the first-line manager is responsible for reaching. The goals included in this accountability statement become the focus of the analysis. If, for example, the first-line manager of a warehouse is accountable for maintaining an inventory not exceeding one million dollars, the warehouse manager's job must be viewed in light of this goal.

An accountability or goal statement should then be used to distinguish between effective and ineffective managers. If the person performing the job consistently reaches these goals without interfering with affiliated functions, the person has to be considered as effective, and the skills possessed are the skills needed to perform the job.

The next step in the job analysis is to observe first-line managers performing their jobs. Observations can be made as part of the regular work day. Past performance evaluations and records of problems with ineffective managers yield additional information about the skills necessary for the job.

Asking effective first-line managers to talk about their skills is another way of obtaining information for a job analysis. Talking with first-line managers about their skills yields information about the job that represents the focus of those currently performing the job. Discussing the job with managers at higher levels will give you information about the job from people with different points of view.

The observations, conversations, and discussions yield information about the first-line manager's job. Before this information can be used in the selection process it must be analyzed, and general statements of the skills needed to function effectively in the job must be made. These statements are actually statements of the selection criteria for evaluating candidates.

In a job analysis conducted by Development Dimensions of one first-line manager's job [1], the following factors were isolated as essential to effective performance:

1. Initiative

2. Identification with a managerial role

3. Planning and organizing

4. Control

5. Leadership

6. Judgment

7. Decisiveness

8. Problem analysis

9. Sensitivity

10. Creativity

The results of this job analysis contain two skills not normally associated with first-line management, initiative and creativity. Normally, first-line managers are thought to be people who function within the confines of a carefully defined performance parameter. The inclusion of these factors suggests the benefit of conducting a job analysis even of first-line management jobs with which you are very familiar.

MAKING JUDGMENTS OF POTENTIAL

Typically, selection decisions for first-line managers include consideration of people who have no experience in management jobs. As a result, you are required to make judgments about a person's potential to develop management skills. Potential may be defined as the ability to develop skills in the future under existing learning conditions.

Since information about current performance as a manager cannot be used in evaluating the effectiveness of inexperienced people, other indicators must be sought. The most frequently used indicators are things a person has done that are similar to management tasks. The assumption is that you can predict how well a person will do a management task on the basis of how that person has done in similar tasks. For example, a person who has planned his or her own work and done it well will most likely do well scheduling work for others. This is a prediction, however; a prediction based on the assumption that scheduling work for oneself and scheduling work for others are similar tasks.

When you use performance of similar tasks as a prediction of potential, you must be able to prove the predictability or relationship. You must, for instance, be able to prove that leadership in nonbusiness situations is a good predictor of later performance as a leader in the business world. The accuracy of judgments of potential can be increased if you identify in advance the indications of potential that you will accept. For example, decide in advance whether getting along with difficult people in the work group as a coworker should be accepted as an indication of interpersonal relationship skills needed as a first-line manager. Specifying what you will consider as indicators of potential before you begin the search will increase your accuracy in making judgments of potential.

While the indications of management potential are numerous, Bray, Campbell, and Grant [2] suggest that seven indicators be closely observed. They are listed in Chart 9.1.

CHART 9.1   INDICATORS OF MANAGEMENT POTENTIAL

INDICATOR	EXPLANATION
Administrative skills	A potentially effective manager currently plans and organizes his or her work effectively, makes decisions willingly, and makes high-quality decisions.
Interpersonal skills	A potentially effective manager currently makes a forceful and likable impression on others, has good oral-presentation skills, leads others to perform, and changes behavior when necessary to reach a goal.
Intellectual Ability	A potentially effective manager currently learns readily and has a wide range of interests.
Stability of Performance	A potentially effective manager currently maintains effective work performance under uncertain or unstructured conditions and in the face of stress.
Work Motivation	A potentially effective manager currently finds the satisfactions of work more important than those of other areas of life and wants to do a good job for its own sake.
Career Orientation	A potentially effective manager currently wants to advance significantly more rapidly than his or her peers, is not as concerned as others about having a secure job, and is unwilling to delay rewards for a long time.
Dependence on Others	A potentially effective manager currently is not overly concerned about gaining approval from superiors and peers.

Considering each of these seven indicators should provide you with a great deal of insight into the management potential of inexperienced candidates.

INTERVIEWING CANDIDATES

The most frequently used method of evaluating candidates for a first-line manager's job is the interview method. In the interview method, you ask the candidates questions, and use the information they provide in response to the questions to make the judgment of suitability for the position. The success of this method of assessment is based on the types of questions you ask during the interview. An example of a question that might be asked is, "What type of planning are you responsbile for in your current job?" Since some candidates are inexperienced, a similar question about planning has to be developed for them. For example, "What type of planning do you feel gets the best results in business?" It is these management-oriented questions that will provide you with the information you need to make judgments about management skills and potential.

Asking Management-Oriented Questions

The first-line manager, interviewing a candidate for a technical position such as key punch operator, might say, "Tell me about the kinds of projects you are involved with currently." The sales manager might say to a candidate for a sales position, "Describe your most successful sale." These questions are focused on and yield information about technical skills. Since you are evaluating candidates for a mangement position, you should ask management-oriented questions. Management-oriented questions should include questions about planning, directing, and controlling.

Since questions about management skills and potential are not a part of everyday conversations, you must give careful consideration to developing management-oriented questions. The questions to be asked about management skills and potential should be thought out before you begin interviewing management candidates. The following sections provide examples of questions that yield useful information.

Questions About Planning

Planning includes goal setting, resource allocation, determining methods, and scheduling. The following three questions will help you learn about a candidate's planning skills.

1. What types of work schedules do you develop with your people?

2. How much detail do you think is important in developing workable plans?

3. Have you found Management by Objectives to be an effective planning method?

To judge the potential of inexperienced candidates, ask

1. In scheduling your own work, what lessons have you learned about planning?

2. Why do you think managers should set goals that are measurable?

3. Do you think Management by Objectives would work in your current work situations?

Questions About Directing

Leading, training, motivating, and staffing are all parts of the management task of direction. Questions like the four following will help you focus the conversation in the interview on this management skill.

1. How would you describe yourself as a leader?

2. What type of training do you give new people in your work group?

3. How do you go about disciplining a person?

4. Where do you find your best people?

To judge the potential of inexperienced candidates, ask

1. How would you describe the best leader you have ever known?

2. If you were a manager, how would you go about training a new person?

3. Have you ever known a manager who you felt really knew how to discipline workers?

4. Where would you look for good people if you were a manager?

Questions About Controlling

The management task of controlling involves following up to see that what you want to happen is actually happening. It is a critical first-line management skill. Questions like the following will help to obtain information about the management skill of controlling.

1. How do you follow up on work assignments?

2. What types of reports do you require your people to make?

3. What is the first thing you do when something has gone wrong?

To judge the potential of inexperienced candidates, ask

1. What type of follow-up on work assignments do you think managers should make?

2. Do you think the types of reports your manager asks you to give are meaningful?

3. When a manager determines that something has gone wrong, what is the first thing he or she should do?

Fifty Percent Failure

Questions about planning, directing, and controlling are directed at eliciting information about management tasks. Perhaps it is because of a lack of such questions that the rate of success in hiring managers is so low. Sampson [3] quotes a study of 55 national companies who measured the effectiveness of hiring decisions over a three-year period. Fifty percent of the people hired for management positions failed. It is quite possible that the wrong questions were asked during selection interviews.

Compatibility or Competency

Asking questions about the management tasks of planning, directing, and controlling will assure you that the interview conversation will go beyond the stage of establishing personal compatibility. It is one thing to be able to say with certitude, "I think I can work with this person," and quite another to say, "I think he or she will make a good first-line manager." The first statement is a statement of compatibility. The second is a statement of competency.

A Written Opinion about the Management Job

Since the opinions a person has about a job greatly influence how that person will perform on the job, you may want to spend some time discussing each candidate's opinions. An interesting approach to getting candidates to express their opinions is the use of the Management Opinion Questionnaire. The Management Opinion Questionnaire consists of 10 open-ended questions. Each question allows the candidates to express their individual opinions about some aspect of management. Prior to conducting an interview with a candidate for a first-line management position, ask the candidate to complete the Management Opinion Questionnaire on page 128. The opinions can then be discussed in the interview.

USING PERSONNEL-SELECTION SPECIALISTS

Middle managers who realize the limitations of the interviewing method in getting the information can turn to personnel-selection specialists for assistance. Among the approaches used by selection specialists are

- Assessment centers
- Paper-and-pencil psychological tests
- Projective psychological tests

Assessment-center Methods

The assessment-center method is a selection method that involves observing candidates as they participate in activities that are similar to the actual on-the-job activities of first-line managers[4]. It is based on the assumption that behavior of candidates involved in these simulated job activities is a predictor of what they will actually do on the job.

MANAGEMENT OPINION QUESTIONNAIRE

Complete each sentence in your own words.

1. My greatest asset as a planner is _____

_____

2. The management control function involves_____

_____

3. The first step in training is _____

_____

4. Organizing a group of people requires _____

5. What I'd look for in an interview with a job applicant is _____

_____

6. In solving management problems _____

_____

7. Reaching decisions involves _____

_____

8. The leadership skills I most admire in managers are _____

_____

9. The best advice I'd give a manager about meetings is_____

_____

10. The best manager I know _____

_____

Job simulations included in the assessment-center method are: in-basket exercises, management games, role-playing interviews or conversations, fact-finding exercises, oral presentations, and written communication exercises. The behavior of candidates for the first-line manager's job is observed in these job-related exercises by assessors who record observations of candidates' behavior. Since the job-related exercises are designed to be similar to the tasks identified by job analysis as being significant in the successful performance of the first-line management job, inferences can more easily be made about future job performance.

An example of a business game used in some assessment centers is Conglomerate. The instructions read as follows: "A conglomerate exists when one organization owns or controls several related or unrelated business enterprises or companies. Your team will be trying to obtain ownership or control over various companies to form a conglomerate or series of conglomerates. Your team will be given a number of stock certificates representing blocks of stock in different companies. Each company has one million shares. The winning team will be determined by the number and type of conglomerates legally held at the end of the session"[4]. Among the skills that are evaluated using the Conglomerate game are risk taking, decision making, and using judgment. Another job-simulation task used in assessment centers is the irate customer phone call. Candidates are informed that they will receive a call from a customer, and they are to play the role of a store manager in answering the call. The irate customer role is played by an assessor who makes the call and records the candidates' responses to the irate behavior. Obviously, this is a great test of tact under stress.

Job simulations like Conglomerate and the irate customer call have the advantages of being job related yet also containing the element of fun associated with such games as Monopoly and the theater.

About the only limiting factor in using this method is the time and money required to conduct an effective assessment center. Professionals conducting assessment centers for organizations insist on beginning with a well-conducted, yet time- and money-consuming job analysis. In addition, middle managers have to be trained to be assessors, and each candidate must be freed for two days to participate in assessment-center activities. Candidates' time also involves money.

Paper-and-Pencil Psychological Tests

If asked to describe the ideal tool for evaluating candidates for first-line management positions, you would most likely say,"This tool should be free from the subjective influence of the person doing the evaluation; it should yield the same results every time it is used and it should not cost too much or take too much time." Paper-and-pencil psychological tests have all these advantages.

Anastasi [5] defines a psychological test as "an objective and standardized measure of a sample of behaviour." The word *objective* refers to the fact that psychological tests measure behavior without the evaluator's subjective influence. *Standardized* refers to the procedural uniformity of test administration and scoring. The phrase *sample of behavior* indicates that predictions made about the person taking the test are based on observations of a small but representative part of the behavior being predicted.

Paper-and-pencil psychological tests for use in evaluating candidates for first-line management positions are plentiful. Tests range from leadership questionnaires to tests of business judgment.

An Example—Dimensions of Temperament

One of the judgments that must be made about a candidate for a first-line manager's job is how well the candidate will direct people on the job. Directing people requires qualities like dominance and tough-mindedness. Tests like Thorndike's *Dimensions of Temperament* (D.O.T.) [6] yield information about these two qualities and eight others. These ten qualities and the behavior associated with them are listed in Chart 9.2.

Psychograph©

An interesting method used to report the results of written psychological tests is the Psychograph©. The Psychograph contains

CHART 9.2 QUALITIES MEASURED BY D.O.T.

QUALITY	EXPLANATION
Sociability	Likes to be with other people, to do things in groups, to be in the middle of things
Dominance	Likes to be in the center of the stage, to speak out, to sell ideas, to meet important people—stands up for rights
Cheerfulness	Seems to feel generally well and happy, satisfied with relations with others; is accepted by others and at peace with the world
Placidity	Is even tempered, easy-going, not easily ruffled or annoyed
Acceptance	Tends to think the best of people, to accept them at face value, to expect altruism to prevail
Tough-mindedness	Is rational rather than intuitive
Reflectiveness	Is interested in ideas, abstractions, discussion, and speculation, in knowledge for its own sake
Impulsiveness	Is carefree, happy-go-lucky, ready to do things at a moment's notice
Activity	Is full of energy, on the go, quick to get things done, able to accomplish a great deal
Responsibility	Is dependable, reliable, certain to complete a task on time, even a little compulsive

a percentile ranking in the 10 interpersonal factors measured by Thorndike's *Dimensions of Temperament*, a percentile ranking in the motivational needs as measured by the *Edwards Personal Preference* test, and a percentile ranking in consideration and structure, the two factors that are indicative of a person's leadership approach.

Percentiles Permit Comparisons

A candidate's score on a psychological test only has meaning when it is compared with scores obtained by effective first-line managers. For example, a score of 56 on a test means nothing unless it is

PSYCHOGRAPH©
(Standardized Test Results)

Name _____ Considered For _____

Prepared For _____ Date_____

NEED STRENGTHS
(Edwards)

PERCENTILE

	10	25	50	75	90	99
Achievement						
Deference						
Order						
Exhibition						
Autonomy						
Affiliation						
Introspection						
Succorance						
Dominance						
Abasement						
Nurturance						
Change						
Endurance						
Aggression						

INTERPERSONAL FACTORS
(Thorndike)

	10	25	50	75	90	99
Sociability						
Dominance						
Cheerfulness						
Placidity						
Accepting						
Tough-mindedness						
Reflective						
Impulsiveness						
Activity level						
Responsibility						

LEADERSHIP APPROACHES
(Leadership Opinion Questionnaire)

	10	25	50	75	90	99
Consideration						
Structure						

compared with the scores of successful managers. When it is known that a person obtaining a score of 56 has a score higher than 98% of the successful managers taking the test, this score takes on meaning.

The percentile, then, is a means of comparing a candidate's score with the scores obtained by successful managers. A percentile score of 25 would indicate that this candidate scored above 25% of the successful managers and below approximately 75% of the managers. The percentile scores on the Psychograph© allow you to compare candidates. A candidate with a score at the 95th percentile on the need for dominance will typically be more dominant than a person with a score at the 25th percentile.

Properly validated and properly interpreted, psychological tests can be a tremendously valuable tool to use in evaluating first-line management candidates. Validation costs money, and some companies have not been willing to spend the money. Proper interpretation also requires that a psychologist become involved in your business so that he or she really understands the first-line manager's job.

Projective Techniques

A projective technique is a method of evaluation in which a person is asked to describe or respond to an ambiguous stimulus of some kind. The best-known example of projective technique is the Rorschach Ink Blot Test [7], in which the person being evaluated is asked to describe a design printed on a card. Since the response to the card requires the person to interpret the design subjectively, it is a very personal response. The ambiguity of the design allows for an expression of individuality. It is this individuality that reveals the management candidate's personality.

The sentence completion test is another type of projective test. In this approach, the candidate is asked to write or verbalize orally a response to an incomplete sentence. An example of an incomplete sentence would be: "Troublemakers should be. . . ." An autocratic person would tend to complete this sentence by saying, "Troublemakers should be punished." A more liberal person might complete the sentence by saying, "Troublemakers should be controlled." The way a person completes the sentence suggests that person's individuality. It is this expression of individuality that allows the psychologist to discover the personality of the management candidate.

Henry and associates [8] some years ago developed a projective technique called the *Thematic Apperception Test*. In this test, the candidate is shown a picture and asked to tell or write a story about it. The first picture in the series shows a picture of a boy looking at a violin. Some people tell a story of a lonely boy deeply involved in his own thoughts; others tell a story of a boy being forced to practice while trying to figure a way to get out of the house. The first story focuses on contemplative thoughts, the second on manipulative thoughts. The stories about the pictures reflect individual experiences and usually reveal a great deal about a management candidate's goals, attitudes, and needs. Other pictures in the series suggest stories of family, friends, and enemies; there is no one "best" story.

The lure of the unknown and the unconscious belief that undefinable spiritual powers actually exist give the projective testing method some of its appeal. Substantive contributions to candidate selection decisions can be made with the use of projective tests, provided the personnel-selection specialists administering the tests understand the first-line manager's job you are trying to fill.

SUMMARY: SPOTTY MANAGEMENT SKILLS

Spotting management skills begins with a consideration of the skills needed to function effectively as a first-line manager. First-line management skills include planning, directing, and controlling work group activities. As a middle manager, you are required to make judgments about the management skills of experienced candidates as well as about the potential of inexperienced candidates. While interviewing is the traditional way of evaluating candidates, many interviews fail because the wrong questions are asked. Personnel-selection specialists can provide some assistance to you through the use of assessment centers, paper-and-pencil tests, and projective techniques, but they only provide answers to questions. Unless you ask management-oriented questions of candidates and selection specialists, you will not get the information you need to make good selection decisions.

REFERENCES

1. Job analysis study results. Pittsburgh: Development Dimensions, 1974.

2. Bray, Doug; Campbell, Richard; and Grant, Donald. *Formative Years in Business: A Long Term AT&T Study of Managerial Lives.* New York: Wiley, 1974, p. 3.

3. Sampson, Richard. *Managing the Managers.* New York: McGraw-Hill, 1965, p. 157.

4. Byham, William. "Assessment centers for spotting future managers," *Harvard Business Review* 48(4): 150–160 July–August, 1970.

5. Anastasi, Anne. *Psychological Testing.* New York: Macmillan, 1961, p. 21.

6. Thorndike, Robert. *Dimensions of Temperament.* New York: Psychological Corporation, 1966, p. 6.

7. Rorschach, Herman. *Psychodiagnostics: A Diagnosis Test Based on Perception.* Berne, Switzerland: Huber, 1942.

8. Henry, William, E. *The Analysis of Fantasy: The Thematic Apperception Technique in the Study of Personality.* New York: Wiley, 1956.

CHAPTER 10

Playing the Role of the Middle Manager

THE ROLE MODEL

A role model has been suggested for you as a middle manager. You have been described as a planner, director, and problem solver. Each middle-management task has been outlined and suggestions have been given for building skills needed to perform these management tasks. Your role as a middle manager has been differentiated from the role of the first-line manager.

It is now time for you to use these ideas in your role as a middle manager. Because you interact with other managers, the role you play is not simply a matter of deciding what you intend to do and doing it. Very likely, different opinions exist in your organization as to the role you should play. Your first-line managers may feel that you should continue to do certain things that you consider as parts of their roles. Top-level managers may resist letting you do some of the things you wish to do. Playing the role of a middle manager as it should be played almost always results in some type of role conflict.

ROLE CONFLICT

Middle managers sometimes say:

"She treats me as if I were still a supervisor!"

"I thought I was supposed to be a decision maker, not a report writer."

"They make the hiring decisions for me."

"I'm not paid to do a supervisor's thinking."

These statements reveal the role conflicts that develop when you as a middle manager expect to be treated one way and are actually treated another. If you give up in disgust and reluctantly accept the role your peers, subordinates, and bosses suggest you play, significant loss of your effectiveness will result. Surrendering your desired role as a middle manager also prevents growth of middle-management skills. If you are unwilling to deal with role conflict, you may never develop your skills as a middle manager.

The Middle Manager's Role As Others See It

Kay [1] suggests some reasons for role conflict in his statements of differing perceptions of the middle-management role. As seen through the eyes of the first-line manager, ineffective middle managers have no real influence because they do not know how to sell ideas to top-level managers. Inflexibility is another word first-line managers use to describe ineffective middle managers. According to Kay, first-line managers feel their bosses rigidly enforce policies and procedures and are unwilling to admit their limitations. First-line managers see ineffective middle managers as people who lack influence, are rigid, and are unwilling to admit limitations.

An equally interesting perception of ineffective middle managers comes from observations made by top-level managers. According to Kay, top-level managers see ineffective middle managers as meddling too much in the decision-making role of top management. Apparently, ineffective middle managers do not make a distinction between the decisions that are theirs and those that are the responsibility of top management. Ineffective middle managers are also cited for making unrealistic demands. Middle managers who make unrealistic demands are unable to accept the limitations of resources. Top-level managers cite meddling in decision making and unrealistic demands as characteristics of ineffective middle managers.

These criticisms suggest that the role of the person in the middle cannot be played without reaction from above and reaction from below. Such reactions suggest that it is up to you to develop and enact an independently formulated role.

Independent Role Formulation

To formulate your role as a middle manager, you should begin with a review of your organization's expectations of you. These expectations are usually stated in a job description. This statement of your organization's expectations has to be your first consideration in formulating your role. Some job descriptions are so well written that reading them gives you a clear notion of the role you are expected to play. Other job descriptions are written by people who do not understand the role of the middle manager; these descriptions only vaguely suggest the role you should play. Regardless of the type of job description available, it should be considered as you independently formulate the role you want to play.

You should also take a look at the roles other middle managers play in your organization. The approaches of different individuals to the middle-management tasks of planning, directing, and problem solving are seldom the same. Considering the accepted variations in the role in your organization should help you formulate a more meaningful role for yourself.

Your experience reporting to different middle managers as a first-line manager should also be considered. As a first-line manager, you most likely reported to more than one middle manager. Since no two people approach the same job in the same way, you undoubtedly have had exposure to more than one kind of middle manager. Some of the things each of the middle managers did you considered effective. Other actions you may have considered ineffective. Your own reactions to the roles played by different middle managers should allow you to make some meaningful differentiations and establish your preferred role.

Knowing the role your boss in top management played when he or she was a middle manager will give you a great deal of insight into your boss's perception of the role you should play. Conversations with your boss and with the other middle managers who report to him or her should also help clarify your boss's expectations.

Your personal goals, your preferred method of operation, and your management skills also must be taken into account. These are the personal elements of your management role. They represent assets that are uniquely yours. Because they are unique, only you can use them in playing the role of middle manager. You must consider these personal assets in formulating your role as a middle manager.

Once you have formulated the role, put it in writing. Include in your written statement the way you want to interact with your boss in top management, with your peers in middle management, and with your subordinates in first-line management. Seeing a written statement of the role you intend to play helps define and integrate these complex relationships. The role statements need not be lengthy.

A regional sales manager's role statement might be, "While I am willing to review plans with top management, I want to plan sales activities in my region with complete autonomy. I intend to give the same autonomy to my district sales managers. When problems develop that my district managers are able to resolve, I expect them to do so. I expect them to bring to my attention the problems they cannot solve."

A production manager's role statement might be, "Once I have accepted production goals from top management, I expect to be able to control the personnel and equipment assigned to me to see that these goals are reached. While I am willing to adjust production goals, I expect that reasonable resources be made available to allow me to make these adjustments."

In formulating your role as a middle manager,

- Consider your job description.
- Take a look at the role other middle managers play.
- Determine your boss's perception of your role.
- Consider your personal skills and goals.
- Formulate your role in writing.

Formulating your role independently helps ensure that you will develop your middle-management skills and permits you to contribute to the effectiveness of your organization. Middle managers who enact the role they independently formulate almost always are successful. The formulated role is a purposeful statement of goals that gives day-to-day activities focus and purpose.

Meeting Role Resistance

As a new middle manager or as a middle manager with a new role, you will most likely meet with some resistance to the role you want to play. The major reason for this resistance is that established managers find adjustment difficult. They tend to resist change and persevere in their behavior. Resistance to making adjustments is particularly prevalent in middle managers who are also middle aged [2]. The familiar, the traditional, and the conventional are preferred to the new, the changed. Almost inevitably, a new role will meet with resistance.

When the role you have formulated for yourself is challenged, you can either make some adjustments in that role or you can quit and find an organization that will let you play the role you have formulated. Alternatively, you can attempt to resolve the conflict. Whenever you can make minor changes in your role to gain acceptance, this should be done. Quitting and searching for another opportunity has some merit but also high risks. The answer seems to be to find a way to resolve the role conflict within your current organization.

RESOLVING ROLE CONFLICTS

In a synopsis of the literature on role playing in the *Handbook of Social Psychology*, Sarbin and Allen [3] suggest a process for resolving role conflict. They indicate that you begin the resolution of role conflict by clarifying for yourself the role you want to play. The next step is to identify the actual role other people want you to play. Once this has been done, the differences between the role you want to play and the role others want you to play can be identified. The reasons these differences exist can then be examined and steps initiated to resolve the conflict.

In resolving role conflicts,

- Know the role you want to play.
- Determine the role others want you to play.
- Identify the differences between the two roles.
- Determine why differences exist and resolve them.
- Recognize partial acceptance of your role.

Knowing the Role You Want to Play

By independently formulating the role you want to play, you have determined how you can best contribute to your organization and how your organization can contribute to your development. Knowing your role is the first step in enacting the role. Because you must play this role in an organization where effectiveness is determined by interdependence, usually the role you want to play will conflict with the roles of others in the organization.

Determining the Role Others Want You to Play

As pointed out previously, the formal role prescribed for you in the organization is usually stated in a job description. No matter how well written the job description is, it is rare that the formal written role is the actual role you will play. Actual roles are suggested by managers at every level by their interactions with you on a day-to-day basis.

The formal, written role (your job description) might suggest that you are responsible for spotting problems. The first time you spot a problem and bring it to the attention of your boss, the reaction you receive will determine whether the formally authorized role should be continued. If your boss is receptive, your formal role as a problem spotter will be reinforced. If he or she is not receptive, you know that problem spotting is discouraged. Pursuing problem spotting as part of your responsibilities under the latter circumstances will result in the surfacing of role conflicts.

Your formal role might suggest that you review and approve your first-line manager's plans. If you do the planning for the first-line manager rather than review and approve, you have changed the actual role you play. Presuming the first-line manager considers planning a part of his or her job, role conflict exists.

The formal job description might suggest that you freely exchange information with other middle managers. If a peer-level manager uses your information against you, your willingness to exchange information in the prescribed manner is reduced. A role conflict between you and another middle manager can develop if you do not accept the role of a free exchanger of information.

The process of determining the role others want you to play should begin with a consideration of your formal job description. Because formal roles are typically not actual roles, day-to-day relationships also have to be considered in determining the roles others want you to play.

Identifying the Differences Between the Two Roles

You have defined two roles, the role you want to play and the role others want you to play. A comparison of these two roles makes the differences obvious.

A middle manager in charge of the production department might define the role this way: a middle manager should run the department but the boss should be available to help if advice is needed. The associates of a middle manager should be willing to cooperate when the goals of the production department and their departments interact. The middle manager's subordinates should develop their own plans, but they are subject to the review and approval of the middle manager.

The people in the organization in which the middle manager works may define this role in a different way. They might say the middle manager should run the department without help and should be able to figure things out alone; otherwise he or she doesn't belong in the job. Associates may feel that they do not need to cooperate, and subordinates may define their jobs as implementers, not as planners. The differences between these two roles are that (1) while the middle manager wants to get help when he or she asks for it, the boss considers asking for help a sign of weakness; (2) while the middle manager views cooperation as necessary, associates are unwilling to provide it; and (3) while the middle manager wants subordinates to plan on their own, they want him or her to do the planning and don't want to risk thinking on their own.

An Example—The Research Department

The people working with the middle manager in charge of research and development might define the middle-management role in these words: the middle manager is responsible for developing new products within the limits of the budget, but working primarily alone with minimal information from other middle managers. They also might feel that each work group should be allowed to function without controls or interference from the middle manager.

The middle manager might consider it necessary to develop new products and improve existing products. While budget restrictions have to be accepted, money should be made available for special products with strong competitive potential.

The middle manager in charge of research and development can be effective only if—as a functioning part of the organization— he or she interacts extensively with other middle managers. The first-line managers in charge of each work group are responsible for assigning projects, developing schedules, and making progress reports. The differences between these two roles are quite extensive. The nature of the departmental goals, the extent of involvement with other middle managers, and the view of how a creative work group should function are all different.

Defining the two roles and comparing the definitions make the differences obvious. Some of the differences can be easily resolved; others require thoughtful consideration.

Determining Why Differences Exist and Resolving Them

You have identified the differences in role expectations. The reasons why these differences exist may be due to any one of the three following causes:

1. The prescribed role has been changed unofficially.

2. There is no prescribed role.

3. Your self-prescribed role is rejected by the other managers.

The prescribed role has been changed unofficially. The difference between the role you want to play and the role others suggest for you may be the difference between the prescribed role and the middle management role as actually performed in the organization. Differences like this usually result from temporary accommodations of role responsibility to meet crises or make up for the lack of skill of a former middle manager. In this situation, you can use the prescribed role to convince others of the role you want to play. In the example of the middle manager in the research and development department, the prescribed role of developing practical as well as creative ideas can be used to change the role first-line managers play.

There is no prescribed role. The differences between the role you want to play and the role others want you to play may be due to the fact that there is no prescribed role for middle managers to play in your organization. The role is left up to the middle managers themselves to work out. The organization has not really decided what the role of middle manager should be. In this situation, the resolution of the differences is up to you. The role you play is a self-prescribed one that you sell to the other managers.

You can change what you do and the way you do it in the organization. It does not require intervention from your boss. It does not require that the personnel department rewrite your job description. You can change your role if you sell the role you want to play to the other people in the organization. Selling consists of pointing out the benefits of the role you desire to the organization, to your boss, and to the other managers.

Your self-prescribed role is rejected by the other managers. The difference in this case may be the difference between the traditional and practiced role and an entirely new role that you propose to play as middle manager. In this situation, you stand alone.

This type of difference is only resolved in your favor if you give the other managers a reason for making an exception for you. The managers believe they should review every decision you make. Their prescribed role requires that they do this, and they have always done it in the past. You must give them some reason for making an exception for you. Once again, the role you play is the role you sell for yourself to the other managers. The reason you give for the role you propose might be a developmental one expressed as: "I need to improve my decision-making skills. Let me make this decision on my own." Another reason might be that you, unlike others, have well-developed skills: "I've been making decisions on matters like these for some time, and I've yet to be wrong. I'd like to make this type of decision on my own."

Acknowledge Partial Acceptance of Your Role

Since people change slowly, complete and consistent acceptance of a changed role is most unlikely. More characteristically, the changed role will sometimes be accepted and sometimes be resisted. Whenever another manager accepts the changed role, acknowledge his or her willingness to let you enact the changed role. Whenever the new role is resisted, point out the benefits of the changed role.

Every time your boss, your associates, or your subordinates deal with you in the way you want them to deal with you, acknowledge this fact. Acknowledge the acceptance of even partial changes until you have convinced others to let you play the role you want to play.

When you want to do your own hiring and your boss agrees to let you hire a first-line manager on your own, acknowledge the fact and point out the benefits of the decision to let you do it on your own. Acknowledge the fact that the middle manager in charge of personnel is finally sharing salary information with you so you can help sell him or her on this portion of your job role. Make others recognize changes in their attitudes toward your self-prescribed role until that role has been totally accepted.

SUMMARY: YOU CAN CHANGE THE ROLE YOU PLAY

Job descriptions, organization traditions, the personal likes and dislikes of top management, and past practices of middle managers all determine to some extent the role you must play as a middle manager. The middle manager's role is seldom so clearly defined that it cannot be changed. Using the role-changing process suggested by Sarbin and Allen [3], you can change the role you play. You can influence the way people within your organization deal with you and the way you deal with them. You can change the role you play as middle manager.

REFERENCES

1. Kay, Emanuel. *The Crisis in Middle Management*. New York: AMACOM, 1974, pp. 21 and 22.
2. Herlock, Elizabeth. *Developmental Psychology*. New York: McGraw-Hill, 1958, p. 461.
3. Sarbin, Theodore and Allen, V. "Role Theory" in *Handbook of Social Psychology*, Vol. II, ed. Gordon Lindzey. Cambridge, Massachusetts: Addison-Wesley, 1954.